Dedication

Joe would like to dedicate this book
to his late and loving sister,
Louise.

Joe Kinnear
Still Crazy

*The Authorized Biography
by Hunter Davies*

André Deutsch

First published in 2000
by André Deutsch Ltd
76 Dean Street
London W1V 5HA

www.vci.co.uk

A catalogue record for this book is available from the British Library

ISBN 0 233 99892 6

Typeset by Derek Doyle & Associates, Liverpool
Printed and bound
in Great Britain by Mackays of Chatham PLC

Contents

Foreword

It was strange going to see Joe again. I'd met him now and again over the years, but not recently. I'd talked to him on the phone, been a guest of his in the directors' box at Wimbledon, followed his career with great interest, watched him on TV, seen him screaming and shouting on touchlines, enjoyed his post-match quotes and observations and noted, as everyone in football had done, how his weight had blossomed over the years. But I hadn't seen him in his own home since I first met him, back in 1972 when I was writing a book about a year in the life of Tottenham Hotspur.

At the time, Joe was the team's dashing bachelor, always in the latest fashions - which in 1972 meant flairs, his long hair well coiffeured, complete with sideboards - driving an MGB sports car, lean and fit, just over eleven stones. He seemed at first rather laid back, so I was surprised to discover how sensible he had been with his money. Despite being so young, just 25, and still living at home with his mother, he'd bought a couple of houses as an investment.

In those days, even players at top clubs didn't earn much money. The basic wage for an established star was £200 a week and they lived in £20,000 mock-Georgian houses on new estates. There were no agents, no regular live matches on TV. Most of them expected to have to find another job, in the real world, once their football career was over.

Joe was my best friend in the team, partly because he was unmarried and had more time on his hands than the married men, although he did have a girlfriend, Bonnie, whom by chance I had already met. She had her own fashionable men's clothes shop, which I used to patronize in the middle of Hampstead village, just opposite the Tube. By the look of Joe and me today, I don't think either of us have bothered very much with clothes, or the idea of being fashionable, for the last 25 years or so.

I asked all the Spurs players in that first-team pool of 1972 what their plans were for the future. Most of them said no, they certainly did not want to become a manager. They had seen at first hand the pressures on Bill Nicholson, their own manager. 'I couldn't do what Bill Nick does,' said Alan Mullery, the team captain. 'I'd end up in the loony bin.' Yet eight of the players from that year, including Mullery, ended up as managers, with varying degrees of success.

Joe was one of those who said he'd like to continue in football. 'I can't imagine a life outside football,' as I quoted him at the time in the appendix to the book. 'I'll be very sad when it comes. I couldn't go and ponce at a lower club, just for the sake of a living. I'd like to stay in football somehow, perhaps as a coach. Financially, I expect to be completely secure when I retire from football. I plan to buy another house every season. I don't know what my actual job will be, perhaps something in fashion. To get experience, I do the odd after-noons in a furniture showroom ...'

That didn't happen, of course. Furniture's loss was Wimbledon's gain. Though in the end, that club's gain was also Joe's loss, when you consider the effects on his health which led to a heart attack and him leaving Wimbledon. But when I went to see him again in the middle of 1999, now recovered, he was looking fit and healthy, and relatively trim. Over the previous few months out of football he had got his weight down from 16 stone to 14 stone. Still a fine head of hair, now going grey round the temples, but with no signs of receding. At 52, he was determined to get back into football, despite what had recently happened to him.

He lives in Mill Hill, in a detached 1930s house with an immensely long back garden, almost the length of a football pitch. In his neat and tidy study he has most of his medals and trophies displayed, including some of his shirts from his Republic of Ireland days, the sort which today you see being sold at Sotheby's. He pointed to a photo of himself at some dinner-jacketed Park Lane gathering from the 1970s along with Cyril Knowles and Bobby Moore. 'I'm the only one still alive. If only just ...'

Amongst his souvenirs is a letter from Reg Kray, sent to him from prison. How had he got that? 'When I took over at Wimbledon, I was asked by the press what the team needed and I said two strong midfield players. They said had I any in mind? I replied, "Yeah, Reg and Ronnie Kray, they'd do for me ..."' All the press picked up this quote and it was used everywhere. 'I then thought oh no, there could be a knock on the door, for taking the piss. But I got this letter from Reg himself, saying he was amused by the quote and wishing me and my family luck.'

It established Joe as a character, always ready with a comment, delivered in his broad cockney accent. His language is still colourful, as it was in the dressing room at Wimbledon. He is also good at embellishing his stories with actions and gestures, putting on faces and funny walks, which also must have endeared him to the Crazy Gang, but alas can't be captured in cold print.

His achievements at Wimbledon, during his eight years as manager, have been admired by everyone in football, from Sir Alex Ferguson onwards. How did he do it, year after year, keeping them not just safely in the Premier League, but often high up, competing for cup honours, yet on measly crowds, sometimes as low as 5,000, and with a miniscule budget? He had to buy cheap, winkling out overlooked material in the lower leagues, polishing them up, fashioning them into diamonds for the bigger, richer clubs to eventually gobble up.

I didn't see all this talent, back in 1972, didn't see young Joe turning out to be such a brilliant manager or such an extrovert, well-loved personality. And despite following his career from afar, I didn't quite know how he'd got from there to here, from Spurs to Wimbledon, or even why he was currently out of work.

So, over the next few months, while he waited for the phone to ring and summon him to the next chapter of his life, he sat down and told me his story, so far ...

Hunter Davies, July 2000

Ron Kray 73338,
Henley Ward,
Oxford House,
Broadmoor Hospital,
Crowthorne,
Berkshire. RG11 7EG.

Monday Morning.
10th February 1992.　①

Dear Mr Kinnear,　I read with amusement your
Quote into Days Sun Newspaper.
I am Quite Wilking to play for you on Saturdays if
you can get Me out. HA HA.

Seriousky though, it was very good as you to speak
Well as my brother Reggie and Me.
I would like to wish you and Wimbredan F.C. and
your faimily all the luck in the World.

Please give your Chairman 'Sam' our best regards.

God Bless,
your friend

(Ron Kray)

PART ONE

Dublin to Tottenham

Chapter One

I wasn't born Joe Kinnear. I was christened Joseph, but I wasn't born Kinnear. I'm not sure if my mother will tell you the full story. It's a fairly sensitive topic. Which I suppose is why it hasn't been talked about. I think some members of my family even now don't like it being mentioned. But today, what happened is commonplace. It happens all the time.

When I was growing up, it didn't bother me, either way, so I never really asked about it. I didn't want to embarrass my mother. All I know is that I was born Joe Reddy in Dublin on 27 December 1946. My father was called Joe Reddy and he worked in the Guinness brewery. Don't know what he did. He was a keen footballer in his youth, so I'm told, played for St James's Gate and other local Dublin teams.

My mother was born Margaret O'Reilly, always known as Greta. My grandparents were strong Republicans. We came from a massive family, on both sides. Whenever I go to a family gathering in Ireland, there are hundreds there. A lot of them seem to be called Doyle.

I was my mother's third child. There were two girls before me. Shirley born in 1944 and Carmen in 1945. Then me. So it was one every year. We lived in Kimmage, and I think also Crumlin, but I haven't got that clear. All my Dublin memories are a bit cloudy. I know I went to a primary school called Larkfield. My earliest memory is of playing football in the street. There used to be street leagues, one street against another. You'd play all day, till it was dark.

I spent a lot of time at my grandmother's house in Leighland Road, my mother's mother. I then went to live with her full time. I didn't really know what was going on. I wasn't told. My mother didn't involve me in anything happening between her and my father. I gather now he was good-looking, a bit of a one for the women, a bit of a rascal, but that's just what I've picked up. I could be wrong.

Whenever the subject came up later, my mother was always a bit vague. I suppose she didn't want to upset me. Or perhaps she was ashamed of her marriage failing. But she never ever said anything to me against my father. That's why I don't have any bad images of him. I just don't remember him, that's all.

Anyway, for whatever reasons, my mother decided she'd had enough of Joe Reddy. I don't remember being called in, or told something or other on a certain day. I just seemed to find myself living full time with my grandmother. My mother had gone off on her own to England, to find work so I gathered, and some sort of place to live.

I don't know how long she was away, a few months, perhaps a year, I don't know exactly. I think I must have been about age seven. Anyway, one day she arrived back at my grandmother's house in Dublin and took me away with her. She later came for my sisters.

I was a bit worried about leaving my school in Dublin, and my friends, and there was a bit of trepidation about what sort of new school I'd go to. But I also remember a feeling of excitement. I'd never been out of Dublin before. Going on a boat to England was a big adventure. We went from Dun Laoghaire to Hollyhead. I thought it was great, going on the boat. We then went to Liverpool and got the train to Watford.

Yeah, Watford. That was where she was living. I don't know how she'd come to land up there. Maybe she had relations. She had managed to get a job. She always had some sort of job in Watford. One of the earliest I remember was manageress of Finlay's, the tobacconist, in Watford High Street. We lived in half a house in a fairly tough area, rented of course. I think the other half belonged to another Irish family. Could they have been some sort of relations?

My mother had got me into a local primary school, Kingswood

Primary. And straight away I was in the school football team. We won the local primary schools' cup and I was the hero. I won my first medal. That helped me to be accepted. So I wasn't aware of any anti-Irish feeling. It was all a doddle and I loved it. Perhaps in the street people did make remarks about 'that Irish family' or 'those Irish bastards', but not at school. Our street was pretty tough. A lot of people had moved up from poor parts of London. But nobody said anything nasty to me at school. I don't recall any animosity.

I then went on to Leggatt's Way Secondary Modern where it was even better. Like the other school, it was sports mad, so I was lucky again. I was good at athletics as well as football. I think 70 per cent of the time and energy in those two Watford schools I went to was devoted to sports.

At Leggatt's Way it turned out that the headmaster, Mr Mills, was also the sports-master, and he was absolutely football daft. He'd heard about my reputation at primary school, so when I arrived it was announced in school how fortunate they were in having an Irish boy come to the school who was good at football. So I was made, wasn't I.

SCHOOL SPORT TALK

Shock-team Chater

CHATER provided the shock of the week when they defeated Harvey-road 5-2 on their own pitch to reach the semi-finals of the Primary Wix Trophy.

Having held Chater to a draw a few days earlier, Harvey-road were tipped as the winners. It looked as if the prophecy would come true when, three minutes from the kick-off, a long ball through the middle caused panic in the Chater defence and the home side scored.

Chater fought back and within a minute had equalised through Alan Jackett.

By keeping wingers Jackett and Langdale well in the game, the visitors began to take command and scored three times in quick succession just before the interval.

The second-half, with the result never in doubt, was comparatively tame and both sides scored once. Chater now meet Ramrage (Luton) for a place in the final.

The county boys' under-15 team made the journey to Southend on Saturday to play Essex, who fielded, as usual, a strong side.

Although the Herts defence played sturdily with Joe Kinnar (Leggatts Way) giving an impressive performance, the home side won with two goals in the first half.

1960 – Joe – wrongly called 'Kinnar' – plays for his school team.

5

He was a diamond, Mr Mills. He'd give us time off school to play and train and he'd come with us for all the matches. Every year, as I went through the school, we won some sort of trophy. And every morning it would be announced that one of the school teams had beaten St Michael's 2-0, or whatever. Then the whole school would cheer.

Those were the days when sport in English schools was taken terribly seriously, when most schools had their own pitches, their own teams, their own local leagues and enough willing masters to give up most of their free time to running the school teams. Now it's all changed. Many school playing fields have been sold off, which is criminal. So he was a diamond geezer, that Mr Mills. I owe a lot to him.

I suppose I must have lost all my Irish accent by then. I don't understand it myself, how it happened, except where we lived there were a lot of real cockneys, who'd moved from London. I must have picked it up from them. People always think I must have been born and brought up within the sound of Bow Bells. I didn't do it deliberately, not as far as I can remember. But by the age of 18, you would have taken me for a pure Londoner.

Chapter Two

Joe's mother, Greta, still lives in Watford. Her Irish accent is totally intact. She is a great talker, sometimes very hard to interrupt in full flow. Like Joe, she has a gift for narrative, and can get carried away with a tale, sometimes losing or improving the odd detail or precise sequence of events, but always entertaining, warm and good-hearted. She can be rather emotional at times, at other times strong and determined. She's had to be, given the life she's led.

We had met before, in 1972, and she remembers that I complimented her on her wallpaper. I have no memory of doing so, but it sounds like me, being creepy. She also remembers me having to go to a garage to get a new battery for my tape recorder. I have never used a tape recorder in my working life, though I often wish I had, as the hours I spent with the Beatles would have proved very valuable. I've always used little red notebooks, filled with millions of badly handwritten words which even I now cannot read. I said she must have confused me with someone else coming to her house, but she says no, it was me.

Her house is not the one she lived in last time I met her, in Queen's Road, where Joe was brought up, but a few streets away. I have never been in a house with so many ornaments on display – literally covering every inch of the walls and floors. There are photos, dolls, statues, trays, religious icons, plates, jugs, cups, saucers, certificates, souvenirs of every sort. And all immaculate. Keeping them clean must take forever. I thought I was a collector, unable to throw anything out, but I have seen nothing like her displays.

She was born in Dublin in 1925, the only girl out of four children, two of whom, twin brothers, died when young. Her father worked in a pork butcher's shop. 'He was a German pork butcher, Hammerman, the best in Dublin, the crème de la crème of pork butchers.' Her mother was a weaver, one of 12 children, all of whom worked in the same linen-weaving firm, Green Mills.

'We lived on the top floor, under the eaves, of a six-storey tenement in Winetavern Street, Dublin. We had no water, no toilet. We had two buckets – one for slops, and one for water. All four of us lived in the one room. It was a very poor upbringing. It's the hidden history of Dublin, which never gets mentioned. Oh I could write a book about it. It should be done ...'

I said that all big cities, in those times, had equally grim tenement blocks, where the poor lived in appalling circumstances. It's been well recorded, in films and books like *Angela's Ashes*. 'Oh no it hasn't. It's been kept secret. But I was determined to get out of it, do better for myself. I didn't want that sort of upbringing. I had a brain. At 12 I ran away, to get away from all that ...'

Where to? 'My aunty. Then I came back again. We were so poor that, do you know, all we ever got at Christmas time as our treat was taken to O'Connell Street to look in the shop windows. That was all. Just to look. My mother would ask what we'd like as a Christmas present – if we were getting a Christmas present, which we weren't. I remember choosing a doll – but when we looked next in the window, it had gone. I was in tears. The most I ever got at Christmas was a bar of chocolate.

'When I was about 10, a great storm blew the roof off the tenement buildings. We were under the eaves of course, so the authorities had to rehouse us. We got a council house in Kimmage.

'I left school at 14 and went to work in a shirt factory, but after about two years I had to stay at home as my mother was very ill and I became the housekeeper.

'I was still just 16 when I went out on a blind date with a girlfriend – and that's how I met Joe Reddy. He was the friend of my girlfriend's boyfriend. I was the fall guy, you might say. No hold on – Joe was my girlfriend's boyfriend. He decided he preferred me instead. That was it. Anyway, it was a blind date.

'He was seven years older and worked as a stoker at the Guinness brewery. He'd played football for Shamrock Rovers, but I didn't really take that in. He lived in Kimmage, not far from our house. His family had originally come from the country, from the west of Ireland. His father had been in the British army, but they didn't talk about that as they were a Republican family. Joe had two sisters, no brothers. He was very spoiled.

'After going out with him for about six months, I fell pregnant. I only did it once. I didn't know anything. I was only 17. His family blamed me for it. I felt so ashamed. I didn't want to marry him and I don't think he wanted to marry me. But at that time, that was it. You had to get married. Everyone forced you. Parents, priests, everyone. We got married in 1944 in St Agnes Roman Catholic Church in Crumlin.

'We moved in with my mother and father, in their house in Leighland Road. It's pronounced Legland, though it should be pronounced in the Irish way. By the time I was 20, I had three children: Shirley, Carmen then Joseph in 1946. All of them were born in The Coombe. That's one of the oldest parts of Dublin, the part which proves you're a real Dubliner. Joseph was seven and a half pounds. They were all difficult.

'We eventually moved out of my mother's house when we got a Guinness house, with a bit of string pulling, which was in Corrib Road in Terenure. It was considered a better area than Kimmage. They all went to the local primary school, Larkfield. It wasn't a Catholic school. That caused a bit of trouble with my mother. It was just the nearest, so I sent them there.

'By this time, my marriage was over. He was a womanizer, which I'd always suspected. We didn't talk about the marriage being over, and the neighbours didn't know. If he met me in the street with the pram, he would walk home with me, like an ordinary father. But that was all. Just keeping up appearances.

'There were millions of couples like us, tied together in unhappy marriages we couldn't get out of. I saw far worse than mine: women beaten up, thrown into the street, their faces blooded. Even if you were married to the biggest bully and drunk, he was the man, he was in charge. You did what he said. Once he has his cap on, he's the man.

'I went to my priest, told him all this, and he said go home, back to your husband. You have to live with him. He never asked me why I wanted to leave him, what the problem might be. He wasn't interested. Divorce or separation was out of the question. But I had a brain. I knew I was at the beginning of life. There was so much I could do, look forward to. So one day, in 1950, I think it was, I said that's it, I'm leaving. I want my own life.

'He got custody of all three children, because I left him, but of course he couldn't look after them. His mother took in the girls. My mother took Joe. That was the arrangement I left.

'I decided to go to England, get a job, make a new life. I had no money of course. All I could get together was £10. That was mainly with selling a coat. I went on a cattle-boat to Liverpool. I sat on the top, outside, in the rain. When I got to Liverpool, I got off the boat the wrong way and came out near a wall where lots of girls were lined up. I didn't know they were the local prostitutes, waiting for the seamen. A young sailor said I was in the wrong place. He told me where I would find lodgings for the night. I stayed two nights in Liverpool. That was enough. I couldn't understand the people, the way they spoke.

'I had no relations living in England. My brother had gone to England, but at the time he was in the British army, serving abroad. I went to Preston. Someone just told me there was work there. I got a job in the Kardomah restaurant. I did very well. I was their best cashier.

'Then I moved to Cumberland, because Gerry had got a job with Taylor Woodrow. They were building the first atomic station, the one they now call Sellafield. I lived in Whitehaven while he worked on the site ...'

Who is Gerry? I asked, though not wishing to spoil the flow. Why Gerry Kinnear, of course, the new man who had come into her life. Where did she meet him?

'I can't remember. I moved round so much, looking for work, doing different things. He moved around as well. We were in Brentford, Essex for a while. Oh, I can't remember all the places now. Anyway we ended up in Watford. Gerry was working on the rebuilding of some shops. That was where Louise was born.

'One day, I got a letter from my mother in Dublin. Joe was probably about six and a half at the time. She said he was running wild, she couldn't control him. He'd set fire to some neighbour's hedge. The shock of it nearly killed my mother. I could tell she was finding it hard to cope.

'So off I went to Dublin. I knocked at my mother's door. She opened it and I said give me Joe. Just put on any old coat, wrap him up warm, I'm taking him now. His father still had custody, you see, so what I was doing wasn't legal. I turned straight round and went back to England.

'Some time later, I can't remember when, I got a letter from my mother telling me that my two girls were in danger of being put into care. Joe's parents couldn't cope any more. They were getting old. So I got neighbours to look after Amelia and Joe and I went off to Dublin to get Shirley and Carmen.

'I met Joe Reddy at the bottom of the road. He said, "Take them, take them, you'll give them a better life." Then he said that if I wanted to come back, he'd take me. "I've always loved you," he said. "You know that. If I had a life to live again, I would still love you." I said no. I was going back to England, with the girls.

'So that's how we all came together, at last. A family of five. I had two girls by Gerry, Louise and then Amelia. He was a very good father to all of them. When I got married to him, I then changed the names of my children from my first husband to the name Kinnear. Just to keep it all simple ...'

Chapter Three

He was a good man, my stepfather Gerry. He was from the North, from Ulster, not the South. He took on all three of us children when we came from Dublin, me and my two sisters, and did well by us. I had a happy childhood, a happy family life.

He had a good job as a printer. Watford was one of the main printing centres for the whole of the UK, producing many of our national magazines and books. I think he was a machine minder for Odhams. I've always looked upon Louise and Amelia as my real sisters. We are all very close.

When my mother told me that me and my older sisters were changing our surname, I didn't mind. It kept it all neat and tidy. I think perhaps she wanted to do it because of her new life. She didn't really want people from Dublin, perhaps her first husband, to track her down. I dunno. But it didn't bother me.

I suppose I did get a bit spoiled, as the only boy amongst four girls. When I started doing well at football, they were all proud of me, and spoiled me even more. I loved it.

My ambition as a little boy was to be a footballer, like many boys, but I didn't expect it. It was just a fantasy. I assumed I'd leave school and with a bit of luck get some sort of apprenticeship in the print. I quite liked history at school, that was about all. I had no time for English and I was hopeless at maths. But now, if I have to work out the odds on horses, I'm brilliant at it.

When I was 14 I got picked to play for Watford Boys. Then I got picked for Hertfordshire Boys, as right half becoming captain of each team. That's when I began to think that I could be a professional footballer, that it wasn't just a fantasy. I saw it all working out. My local team, Watford, who had recently come up from the fourth to the third division, would be bound to give me a trial. Then they'd offer me an apprenticeship. They were my club, my local little club. It seemed obvious. I had no grand ideas of playing for a big city club. Watford was the height of my ambition.

I was asked to go for a trial. It seemed to go okay and I thought good, I'm all set to take off. I wasn't called for a second trial. But that didn't really worry me, till a letter arrived in the post. It said thanks – but no thanks. They had taken on quite a lot of new young players the previous year, that was the story. They were taking just two or three apprentices this year and they already had the ones they wanted. They took on some who had played with me in the Herts Boys team. I always thought I was better than them. And I had been captain of the team, after all. So I was absolutely devastated.

It had all seemed plain sailing, that I would go to Watford. I hadn't thought of anything else. Up to the moment that letter came, I had assumed not just that they would offer me an apprenticeship, but I had worked out dates and holidays and which day I'd be reporting for training. All my teachers and coaches had said I was a certainty. I'd been in the local papers, as a schoolboy star, expected by all to do well. My whole world caved in.

Looking back, having gone through such things myself from the other side of the fence, I know how hard it is. I've had to turn down kids many times. But it was the way it was done. Nobody explained, nobody pulled me aside, nobody said sorry, son. I still think that was bad, just sending a formal letter. I never did that, I always gave them a reason.

At Wimbledon, I'd often have 30 kids who had come especially from Scotland, Ireland and Wales – all of them expectant. I'd discuss with Terry Burton, Ernie Tippit or Roger Smith who were the best kids, the ones we were going to take, but I'd tell all the other ones personally we weren't taking them. I always told them my story – that I was rejected as a kid, I didn't make it at 15, I was turned down by a third division club. I said I'm living proof that you can still make it. So go away and prove me wrong. The ones we did think were quite good, and might improve, we always kept tabs on them. If they went on to Hartlepool or wherever, we'd keep an eye on their development.

No one knew when I was 15 if I would develop or not. You are always taking a chance. But all the same, I would have taken a chance on me, captain of those two teams. Watford might of course have had budget problems, which I didn't know about, or perhaps they felt strong in certain areas at the time. One of the things you are always concerned about as a coach is where you are weak. This can make you not keep on the best player in your youth team, because he's a forward – unless of course he's really a bit special – but you'll take a reasonable full back because you know your defence is poor. But it still bugs me now, after all these years, that they said no the way they did. I was shattered.

Nobody else came along. And I didn't try another club. I thought if Watford don't want me, who will? That's it. But what do I do now? At the end of the school year, I wasn't joining a football club, as I'd expected. I had to start looking for some sort of job.

My stepfather fixed me up with one, in the print. He got me an apprenticeship at Odhams. I worked in one of their subsidiary companies, Witherby's in Carey Place, Watford. I think they were part of Odhams at the time. They did books, mainly atlases. I helped the lino-type operators, who were working on big Heidlebergs. As a first-year apprentice, I did things like ink the rollers and take proofs to people. I also had to go to nightschool, at Watford Poly, one night a week. I started on £2.50 a week. I enjoyed it – and I knew I'd done well. It was good to get an apprenticeship in the print. They were hard to get.

I'm not sure how long I'd been working there when out of the blue I got a letter from St Albans City. A bloke called Dick East had been at my Watford trial and was sorry I hadn't been taken. He asked if I'd like to come along and train with the team, see how it went. He was their manager.

St Albans were an amateur club, founded in 1908, who played in *the Isthmian League. They had five international players – all amateurs of course. So I went along, joined them in training, and they asked me to play for them. By the age of 16, I was in their first team. Still working of course. I'd go training with them two evenings a week, after work.*

ST. ALBANS CITY FOOTBALL CLUB

Founded 1908

Colours :
BLUE AND GOLD

Ground and Dressing Rooms (No Correspondence):-
CLARENCE PARK
ST. ALBANS
Tel. : St. Albans 53699

Members of: The Football Association   The Herts Football Association   The Isthmian League

Hon. Gen. Sec.
H. Stacey
75 High Oaks
St. Albans
Telephones
St. Albans 54878

President:-
A. B. Hobbs, Esq.

Chairman:-
D. L. S. Rand Esq.

Hon. Treasurer
W. G. Marriner
6 Ridgewood Drive,
Harpenden, Herts
Telephone: Harpenden 5550

2/8/62

Dear Sir,

We would like to offer you a trial game on Tues. evening next at Clarence Park. Could you please arrange to be there at 6.30 p.y and ask for Dick East at the dressing rooms.

Yours sincerely,

1st TEAM SEC.

1962: Joe gets offered a trial with amateur club, St Albans City, after being turned down by Watford

I played right half, as I'd done at school, and for Watford Boys and Herts. I had bundles of energy in those days. I played a sort of Roy Keane role, all over the midfield, up and down. I was very skinny, just ten stone. I could run for hours, no problem. Those were the days.

Although it was an amateur club, you got expenses. The captain would be given the money, in cash, and would go round after each match shoving a few quid in your boots. I got £2 a game. It was officially expenses, to cover your petrol. I didn't have a car of course. But I was pleased: it doubled my wages. It was good fun, playing for them, all very relaxed. I thought my career was over before it had begun, so I had no need to get all tense or nervous. I just enjoyed myself.

I suppose with some people, being rejected by Watford would have made them more determined to succeed. It didn't have that effect on me. I'd given up all hope. There was none of this 'I'll show them, I'll bounce back', I didn't think like that. I thought, 'My future is being a printer, plus I'll be an amateur footballer in my spare time, doing it for fun.'

I suppose what I did have on my side, even at that age, playing as an amateur, was that I was a good worker. I had the right attitude to work. If I was told to be at a certain place at a certain time, even if it meant two hours and six buses, I'd always be there on time. Not all 16-year-old lads have that attitude.

At the end of the season, Dick East said that a guy called Dick Walker had been watching me. I said who's he? He says he's only chief scout of Tottenham. I said you mean Spurs, what has just won the Double? I couldn't believe it. They were the top team in the country, the one everyone wanted to play for. He said yeah. They wanted to know if I would come and train with them during my two weeks' holiday from work, during the summer.

I had to report to Cheshunt, which was where Spurs had their training ground at the time. I turned up on the day I was told, expecting I'd be on my own, the only boy having a trial that day. That's what I really thought. My own personal trial. So I was amazed when I got there to find there were about 60 other boys there.

Masses of them, and masses of coaches with clipboards, all bustling around. Eddie Bailey, the assistant manager, was there, Cecil Poynton, Johnny Willis, Jack Cox, Sid Tickeridge. Probably about 10 coaches, all with clipboards and whistles. Bill Nicholson was also there, walking round. We all stood about, all the boys, not knowing what was going to happen.

1963: Joe gets offered a trial by Spurs

We got put in groups, team A or B or whatever, with different coloured bibs. Then we started playing games. About five games were going on, all at the same time. We stopped for lunch, a free lunch, which was good. We got a sandwich, an apple and a cup of tea. Then in the afternoon we were put in different groups. At the end of the day they said thanks for coming, see you tomorrow.

That first day, I was told to play right back, which I'd never played before. They said they had someone they were looking at in my

Kinnear signs 'pro' for Spurs

AN 18-year-old Watford lad finishes work as a printing apprentice today (Friday). On Monday he starts a new job—as a full-time professional with Tottenham Hotspur Football Club.

He is full-back Joe Kinnear, captain of the Herts Youth F.A. side, and skipper of Spurs' under-18 team.

Joe lives at 112 Queen's Road, Watford, and has for the past three years been working for Witherby's, the printers, in Carey Place, Watford.

After two years with the White Hart Lane Club as an amateur, Joe signed paid forms on Thursday night. Today he goes into full-time training alongside the household name players Jimmy Greaves, Alan Gilzean, Cliff Jones, Maurice Norman, Peter Baker and Ron Henry.

With him at White Hart Lane will be his old Leggatts Way School pal, Roy Lowe, who has already made the Tottenham first team.

Kinnear's ambition, of course, is first team football. He has already had 20 games in the Metropolitan League side and has trodden the famous Tottenham turf in a great number of under-18 floodlit matches.

An ambition which did not materialise for Joe was his longing to wear Watford's colours, although he did have a trial with them. Arsenal, Chelsea and Fulham also tried to obtain his services.

He came to Watford from Ireland at the age of six and played for Watford and Hertfordshire boys.

Kinnear, who plays outside-right for the Watford Sunday League XI (he plays on Sundays for Bournehall Press) and for the Herts County Sunday XI, was spotted by Tottenham when playing for St. Albans City

1965: Joe signs for Spurs

group who was a right half, so I'd have to be right back. I thought that's not going to help my chances, playing out of my position. Then I thought sod it, I'll just bomb forward when I get a chance. Which I did. I was bombing past the right half and linking up with the right winger.

This went on for a week, at the end of which there were only about a third of us left. The other 40 or so had gone during the week, been told one by one not to come back, thank you very much. So in the second week it was just 16 of us. I didn't have much hope. I thought it's going to be the letter in the post again. But to my surprise, they asked me if I'd like to play for their youth team, as an amateur. I'd still be working, but they'd pay my travel expenses. So in August 1963, I signed for Spurs.

For the first game I played in Spurs' youth team, I had to be up at 6.30 to get a train from Watford Junction to Euston. Then I caught a train to Manor House, then a bus to White Hart Lane. All Spurs gave me was a bus pass. I had to pay for the trains.

I spent two seasons with the Spurs youth team. I trained at Cheshunt on Tuesdays and Thursdays after work, then played on Saturdays, in the same team as those boys who were proper Spurs apprentices. These were the one who had been taken on as full-time apprentice footballers at 15, which I'd missed out on. Some of them did think they were a bit special, superstars compared with me. Which was true. They'd played for England Schoolboys, Scotland Boys. They weren't all that impressed by someone who had only made Herts Boys and been turned down by Watford FC.

I remember a kid called Stevie Pitt who was considered the boy wonder. Everyone said he was brilliant, he'd do really well, but he never really made it. He went on to Colchester. Last time I heard, he was working at Heathrow airport. Keith Weller was also there at the time, and he did go on to do well.

[Keith Weller played 19 times for Spurs, then Millwall, Chelsea and Leicester, earning four England caps along the way. Last heard of in the USA, working as a driver for a TV company.]

We had a very good youth team. We went to Holland in May 1965 to play in an international youth tournament. There were 10 *clubs taking part, including Arsenal, Cannes, Ajax, Sparta, Fortuna Düsseldorf. We played on Feyenoord's ground. Johan Cruyff was playing – and we beat his team. We played Arsenal in the final and beat them 1-0 to win the cup. Keith Weller was in that team, and Jimmy Pearce, Tony Want, Roger Hoy, Neil Johnson, John Sainty, Taffy Collins and Deric Possey.*

As youth players, or apprentices, we had to do a lot of the dirty jobs like cleaning up the first-team dressing room after training, when they'd finished. We had to knock on their door, wait till some-one replied, then ask politely if they were ready for us to come in and clean up. You felt like Oliver Twist: 'Please Sir, can I have some more?'

Johnny Wallis was in charge of us and he'd come in afterwards and check we'd done the work. He'd stand in the doorway, look round, then rub his finger along the top of the doorframe. He'd hold up his dirty finger and say, 'Who's supposed to have done this?' Then he'd walk out. We'd all say bloody hell, whose fault was that? We'd rush around, cleaning all the doorframes. He'd then return, and check something else, like the showers, or the khazi. He really would look into the shithole to make sure we'd cleaned it. We'd all be standing there, waiting, dying to get away to catch a bus or train. He'd keep us till he was satisfied. Then he'd say, 'Okay. See you tomorrow.' And we'd run like hell.

But once away from the training ground, I felt like the King of Watford. What. Playing for Tottenham Hotspur! On match days, you had to wear your Spurs blazer, whether you played for the first team or the third team or the youth team. It had a Spurs crest on, and you wore it with a Spurs tie, a white shirt and grey slacks. I used to wear it all the time. Even if I just went shopping in Watford. I'd go up and down the high street, whether it was a match day or not. I was saying look at me everyone, I play for the famous Spurs, don't I. I was turned down by bloody Watford. It felt brilliant.

When I got to 18, Eddie Bailey and Bill Nick called me in and said they thought I had a future. They were offering me a two-year contract as a professional.

I said I had to think about it. I'd done three years as an appren-

tice printer and was now on £6 a week. I had a secure future. What security had I as a footballer? Spurs were a very big club. After two years, I might be chucked out and never make it. I asked them what chance they thought I had. Bill said he could promise nothing, but I had a realistic chance, if I continued to progress at the same rate.

I went home and told my mum. She said go for it. It's what I'd always wanted to do, hadn't I ...?

Chapter Four

I signed full professional forms for Spurs in February 1965, two months after my 18th birthday. I was on £20 a week. I still had a long trail to get from my home in Watford each day to the Spurs training ground at Cheshunt, though eventually I got a lift with another player, two years older than me, Roy How who lived in Watford. I chipped in for the petrol.

I started in the third team, in what was called the Metropolitan League, against teams like the Metropolitan Police. They were real tough outfits, very physical. After about four or five games I got promoted to the reserves, and found myself playing with some of Spurs' big stars, some who had played in the 1961 Double Team, then won the FA Cup again in 1962, and the European Cup Winners' Cup in 1963. They were legends. Spurs have never had a team like that, before or since.

Right from the moment when I joined Spurs, I'd found myself rubbing shoulders with these famous international players – Danny Blanchflower of Northern Ireland, Dave Mackay, Bill Brown and John White of Scotland. John White got killed of course by lightning in July 1964, while playing golf at Enfield. Mel Hopkins, Cliff Jones and Terry Medwin all played for Wales. Then the English internationals included Jimmy Greaves, Ron Henry, Tony Marchi, Maurice Norman, Bobby Smith, Les Allen. Around the time I became a full pro, Pat Jennings, Alan Gilzean and Alan Mullery were signed. So that was more international stars. You couldn't get moving for them. Then there were people like Peter Baker and Ron Henry, and Terry Dyson

*who had scored two goals in the Spurs European Cup Winners'
triumph.*

*Some of them played in the reserves with me from time to time.
Bill Brown was getting on a bit and alternating with Pat Jennings as
first-team goalie. But as a reserve, you weren't quite on equal terms.*

JOE KINNEAR... Selectors must

remember this starlet's name

— by —
JAMES CONNOLLY

FOR Joe Kinnear, 19-year-old Dublin-born wing half, there could be a bright football future with Spurs. From dour, uncompromising manager Bill Nicholson, he earns this praise : "He has speed and ability and looks a good prospect."

Like every other promising youngster at Spurs he has been warned by Nicholson that there is no short cut to success.

It needs the dedication and rigorous self-discipline that men like Chelsea boss Tommy Docherty, and Johnny Carey, Nottingham Forest chief, showed as players.

Kinnear has done well to become an established Spurs reserve and an occasional first team substitute. He now dreams of a senior place that could bring his heart's desire, a cap for the Republic of Ireland.

Young Joe, who left Ireland when he was only six years old, still goes back to Dublin every year to see his grandmother. "It is a visit I look forward to all the year round," he says.

of junior honours. He was a member of the Spurs team that won the international youth tournament in Holland last year.

He has captained his school—Leggatts Way, Watford, near London—and went on to lead Watford boys and Hertfordshire boys.

Three years ago Kinnear, then a full back, joined Spurs as an amateur. He signed professional almost a year ago. They don't rush things at White Hart Lane, but by the end of last season Joe was a regular reserve team member. He was converted to wing half this season.

"Spurs have always been my club," he told me. "I followed them as a boy and I admired the football that Danny Blanchflower played. Watching him taught me something.

"I must be lucky. Spurs are the only club I would ever have wished to play for . . . and

"Every young footballer wants to play for his country—and I am no exception. But first I have to succeed with Spurs before the selectors will even know I am around.

"My father never played professional Soccer, but like my mother he was ready to help me try to make a go of it.

"Because of his work my father doesn't get much opportunity to see me play, but mother comes along whenever she can. I have four sisters so her chances, too, are limited.

Lucky

"I know that I have had the lucky breaks getting to Spurs. But I honestly feel that with their training and coaching I have improved.

"With the help and experience of Mr. Nicholson and his staff behind me, I hope that I will progress further.

"But I appreciate that to get anywhere in this game you have to work hard. And I intend to. After all this is the career I most wanted. Now it is up to me."

They were sort of slumming, when they played with you in the stiffs, or were recovering from injuries. But after a year in the reserves, I started travelling once or twice with the first team. They didn't have lots of subs on the bench in those days, so you just travelled for the experience. Bill would take one or two younger players to away games, just to let them see what it was like.

The next stage was actually training with the first-team squad. That sort of just happened. There was nothing said officially. I didn't get a rise or anything, I was still on my £20 a week. I felt so excited when this happened. I was in awe of them all. They'd done every-thing. Just to get stripped off with Dave Mackay was amazing, or train alongside Cliff Jones. He'd just been picked for a world XI. I can't remember what it was for, but he was there on merit. He was the best winger in the world at that time, no question.

When I was with them all in the dressing room, getting ready, I just kept quiet. I listened, soaked it all up. When you're an estab-lished player, you can take part in all the chat. But when you're new or young, you just listen. I remember the banter as always being very comical.

Danny Blanchflower was a very decent man, but quiet compared with Dave Mackay. When Danny left, I got his number 8 peg and training kit. Jimmy Greaves was a law unto himself. He was Spurs' top scorer, year in year out, the greatest finisher Spurs ever had. I didn't see him drinking a lot, at that time, but he wasn't exactly a keen trainer. But Mackay was my real hero, the greatest player I ever played with, and I went on to play with quite a few. He had the lot: flair, imagination, great tackler, leadership. He was such an inspira-tion, the Governor, off and on the pitch. Bill Nick later told me he knew he could never find another player to replace Dave Mackay.

He used to do tricks in the dressing room, such as juggling an orange on each foot, in turn, then he'd flick it up and catch it on the back of his neck. They were always doing these sort of games in the dressing room, then making bets with each other that they couldn't do it – people like Jimmy Greaves, Cliff Jones, Alan Gilzean.

One of the regular tricks was to flick a half crown up in the air with your foot and shout 'Which pocket?' If the other person shouted, 'Left pocket', you had to catch the coin in the left pocket of your shirt; if they said right, then the right pocket. If you failed, you had to buy the other person a drink or pay him a few quid. Dave Mackay could even land the coin on his eyes. 'Which eye?' he'd shout. He'd catch the coin on his forehead, then stand there, letting it slide down on to the appropriate eye.

One day Cliff Jones was trying this trick. But he caught the coin on the bridge of his nose, not his forehead, and it split it wide open. He had to go into the treatment room to stop his hooter from bleeding. He got some stick for that.

Dave Mackay took a liking to me, even though I was just a young kid. So that was good for me, helped me to get into things, feel part of the team, part of the dressing room. I used to go racing with him. It was through Dave I got into horses.

In training though, he'd kick me as he'd kick everyone else. All our training was for real. Practice matches certainly weren't like friendly matches. Everyone got stuck in, always very competitive. Today, in a training session, a coach will shout, 'Don't put your foot in, go steady, save all that for Saturday.' But in those days Eddie Bailey would stop a practice game and give you a bollocking. 'Are you gonna get your foot in or not?' The philosophy has all changed today. I suppose it was partly to do with the fact that Spurs had so much talent, so many good players available. It was also the sort of footballers they had. In training or in a real game, they were buccaneers who just went out on the pitch to enjoy themselves.

Chapter Five

In February 1966, exactly a year after I signed as a full professional, I thought my chance had come at last, to make my first-team debut. I travelled with the team to an away match against Blackpool. Two young players went with the first team, me and Neil Johnson. I thought I'd get a game that day, as the signs seemed good, but I didn't. I was thrilled to be with the first team, but disappointed not to be picked. I tried not to show it of course. I watched the game from the stands. It was exciting just looking around, at the stands and the crowd. Blackpool were still a big club in those days with a famous history.

A few weeks later, on Good Friday, 8 April 1966, I eventually made it, in a home match against West Ham United. I didn't know till almost the last moment whether I was playing. The names of 13 or 14 had been pinned up from which the 11 would be picked. All of us had to be there, two hours before kick-off. Eddie Bailey told me I had a chance, but it wasn't till the team-sheet went up that I knew I was playing.

Cyril Knowles was left back that day and I was right back. Ron Henry had been the left back in the Double team, with Peter Baker at right back, but Peter Baker had returned to South Africa. I had butterflies before the game, terrified I'd let the team down. I wanted to do well, so I'd be kept in. When we started, I just concentrated on my own game. It was a full house, being a London derby, with a crowd of over 50,000.

19-year-old back has another League chance

SPURS DEBUT FOR KINNEAR

Clayton out for West Ham match

By VICTOR RAILTON

JOE KINNEAR, 19-year-old right-back from Dublin, is the latest Spurs starlet to make a first team debut. He plays in the big London game against West Ham at White Hart Lane to-morrow.

Spurs, who have slipped in recent games, plan to blood several of their promising youngsters during the rest of the season. It's the second time Kinnear, who left Dublin at the age of six for Watford and was spotted playing for amateurs St. Albans City, has been awarded a League debut.

He was due to play against Blackpool last month but a foot injury sustained in Spurs gymnasium forced him to pull out. Now fully recovered, he steps out to mark Hammers left winger John Sissons at the expense of John Collins, another talented Tottenham

Newspaper coverage of Joe's first team debut, 8 April 1966.

In the West Ham team was John Sissons on the left wing and Harry Redknapp on the right wing. Brian Dear, or Stag as he was called, was centre forward. He got a hat trick. West Ham stuffed us 4-1. Despite that, I kept my place and was in for the next seven games, till the end of the season.

I felt by then I'd made it, that I was going to become a first-team player, but you never knew with Bill Nick. He liked to keep you on your toes, fighting for your place. Bill was a perfectionist, and his Double-winning team had been near-perfect. We felt a bit inferior to them, and he probably made us feel that way. Bill would stop a training game, just to make you do something properly, or do it again till you got it right. He'd rant and rave if you did things badly. During a practice game, he'd run beside you and tell you to 'caress the ball' – words you never hear today.

28

Eddie Bailey, as assistant manager, was the other main man. He was a typical cockney character, a cheeky chappie, effing and blinding. Bill Nick was more the dour, silent Yorkshireman. But Eddie was a good coach. 'Do the simple things quickly', that was one of his favourite instructions, bellowing it in your ear'ole.

It was still the era of the old-fashioned leather ball, which was like a lead weight. Bill had been brought up to trap the ball under your foot, under your studs. That was what he insisted on, the correct way. But times were changing and new methods were coming from the continent, and also newer, lighter balls. All the same, he still made us trap the ball his way. He'd stop us bringing it down on our instep. He maintained that if you made a mistake, and the ball bounced off you, you gave it away. By trapping it under your foot, you kept control. That was the theory, the standard practice at the time – trap the ball, push it and run. I would have taught the same way, I suppose, if I'd been a coach at the time.

He also had his own theories about heading. I can still hear him shouting, 'Throw your eyes at the ball'. He had no need of course to teach heading to someone like Gilly (Alan Gilzean). We practised crossing to Gilly for hours, and he'd score every time. He was the best header of the ball I ever met. You couldn't teach him anything about heading. He was an absolute natural.

Gilly was also about the only player I have ever met who was not in love with the game. Every footballer is, even when they moan and groan, get fed up and threaten to pack it in. All players have been in love with football all their life, it's what they've always wanted to do – and it's come true. But not with Gilly. He had no love of football, no real interest in it. He did his training okay, usually the minimum, then that was it. Football was just his job. When he left Spurs, Gilly cut himself off completely. No one I know ever heard from him again. Most unusual.

Playing with Cyril Knowles was a joy. I would rate him about the best left back I've ever seen. He was a terrific crosser of the ball, and could do it on the run better than most left wingers. He was about the first of the overlapping full backs. He should have got a bagful of England caps. In the dressing room, he was the main piss-taker, winding people up, especially poor old Ralph Coates, who arrived at the club from Burnley.

Having kept my place till the end of the season, I was very hopeful at the beginning of the next season, 1966-67. I played as right back in our summer tour of Spain, but when the season began, Phil Beal was given the position. He played the first three games, then I was brought back and he was moved to right half. I played eight games, then ruptured my thigh in training, so Phil came back to right back. That's how it was for the first half of that season: me and Phil competing for the same place. It was all very friendly.

I got in for a Cup match, the third-round tie against Millwall in January. We got through it after a replay, with Gilly scoring the winner. But what changed my luck was some bad luck for Phil. He broke his arm against Manchester City in February and was out for the rest of the season. I got his place and stayed as right back for the duration. In the end I played 20 first-team league games and seven FA Cup games. We finished 3rd in the league – on the same points as Notts Forest who were 2nd – which was the best we'd done since 1963 when the Double team were still around.

But of course the big excitement was the FA Cup. I'd chosen a good season, hadn't I, to get established in the first team. I'd only been in the first team for a year when in April 1967 we beat Notts Forest 2-1 in the semi-final at Hillsborough. Jimmy Greaves and Frank Saul got our goals. It meant we were to meet Chelsea at Wembley in the final. There was a brilliant atmosphere during the weeks leading up to it. Not just at White Hart Lane, but everywhere you went in London, people were talking about it.

The week before, we all went to a dinner at the Hilton Hotel, an Anglo-American Sporting Club event. It was a boxing club, which put on big posh dinners. They'd invited both the Cup Final teams so we found ourselves sitting at the same table, opposite the Chelsea lads. I don't think they'd meet like that today. Terry Venables, who had joined us the May before, had of course played for Chelsea. He knew most of their players already, so we were all soon chatting

Charges to pay

RECEIV +COL +⊁   TS 701   OFFICE

No.
OFFICE STAMP

TELEGRAM

Prefix. Time handed in. Office of Origin and Service Instructions. Words.

20 MAY 67

HARROW
MIDDX

At
From
By   ⊁1108 9.8 WATFORD 29

At
To
By

=JOE KINNEAR SPURS DRESSING ROOM WEMBLEY

STADIUM WEMBLEY

=CONGRATULATIONS JOE YOU DESERVE IT THE LUCK OF
THE IRISH IS WITH YOU GOD BLESS YOU =MUM AND
DAD AND SISTERS

For free repetition of doubtful words telephone "TELEGRAMS ENQUIRY" or call, with this form
at office of delivery. Other enquiries should be accompanied by this form, and, if possible, the envelope.   B or C

and joking. The Cup itself was there, on show at the dinner. I remember looking at it and wondering if it would be ours or Chelsea's.

We spent the night before the final at the Hilton Hotel in London. I roomed with Terry Venables as I usually did. We all went to the pictures the night before to relieve the pressure. Can't remember what we saw, but Eddie Bailey took us. Then when we got back to the hotel and there was a strict curfew, everyone had to go straight to their rooms. I barely slept.

On the way to Wembley, I remember sitting on the bus looking out at all the crowds waving at us, and thinking Christ, I hope I don't let them down.

It was the first Cup Final in which a sub was allowed. They'd come in during that season, but not reached a Cup Final. Bill therefore had the problem of who to leave out and make sub. In the end he decided to leave out Cliff Jones, keep him on the bench. He put in Frank Saul instead. Saul was one of the unsung heroes of Spurs who had come right through the youth teams – and he got the winning goal. Jimmy Robertson got our other goal. We won 2-1.

I was the youngest player on the pitch, aged 20, and I got made Man of the Match. To this day, whenever I meet Bill Nick, he says, 'That was your best ever game, if ever anyone had their day, that was your day.' I often watch the video of that game: it's in black and white of course and the TV coverage is terrible, laughable, really compared to today. Ken Wolstenholme is doing the commentary. He'd done the World Cup Final at Wembley only the year before, and came out with his famous words, 'They think it's all over – it is now.' In our Cup Final, he goes on all the time about 'there goes young Joe Kinnear'. I laugh every time I watch it.

The game itself went in a flash. I can't actually remember any of the incidents. On the video, I can see myself putting my arms round Terry Venables and Dave Mackay afterwards, all emotion drained, but at the time I wasn't really aware of doing it, or of doing anything.

I remember talking to John Hollins as we came down the steps from the royal box, having got our medals. He says, 'Let's have a look at yours.' They were identical on one side – but on the other side, one said 'Winners' and one said 'Runners-up'. John says, 'I hope I'll come back as a winner next time.' I can still see the disappointment on his face.

In that video, there's a shot of me after the match, with socks down, pads off. I'm just staring up at the crowds, looking at nothing, in a daze. Then there's the usual dressing room stuff, sitting in the bath with buckets of champagne, pouring it over each other's heads.

It stood me in good stead, being in a Cup Final so young. I realized immediately afterwards that it had all passed me by, as if I'd been in a daze. I told myself that if there's ever a next time, I'll take it all in more slowly, savour it more carefully.

My winning bonus for the Cup Final came to £500. It was like winning the pools. My two-year contract had been for £20 a week, plus bonuses, but after about a year, when I'd got into the first team, I'd been upgraded to £40 a week. With bonuses, because of the winning run, I suppose at the time of the Cup Final I was averaging £60 a week. So getting that £500 bonus for winning the Cup, that was a huge amount.

I also made a bit of extra money. I'm not sure if I should admit it, even now, looking what happened recently to the Leicester City players. Everyone knows there have been fiddles on Cup Final tickets. For decades, I should think, back to when it all began. As a player in the Cup Final, we were allowed 100 tickets each. We had to pay for them, the full cover price, out of our wages. But what you did was sell the ones you didn't want to the touts. There was Johnny the Stick, One Arm Lou and Fat Stan. They were all real characters, as much part of the Spurs scenery as the players. Jimmy Greaves was very friendly with one of the touts, a real Spurs fanatic. He used to sleep in Jimmy's Spurs shirt.

All season they'd been hanging around, getting any spares from the players, which they'd flog on to punters who couldn't get tickets. Spurs were getting full houses of 50,000-odd for all our Cup games. The tout would pay you double for any spare tickets, in cash, then sell them on for, I dunno, four times, ten times, whatever he could get.

It was a recognized perk for the players, considered normal by everyone, what you did, part of having a successful Cup run. It's the only illegal thing I've ever done in football, but it didn't seem it at the time. As a young player, getting into the first team, you just followed what the older ones did. And as a young player, the money was more important to you – because you were earning a lot less than the stars.

I think some players sold almost all their allocation. But as it was my first Cup Final, and I didn't know if I'd ever be in another, I kept 40 tickets for myself, to give away to my family and friends. There were cousins I'd never heard of in Ireland, all saying they were coming to the game. So I just sold 60 to the touts. I did worry, at the time, about selling the 60. In a way it didn't seem right, but then everyone did it.

So I did well out of the Cup Final. Probably ended up with about £2,000, at the end of the season. I gave £500 to my mother, gave my four sisters £30 each and a new outfit, bought my grandmother in Dublin a TV and an armchair, bought myself a Corsair and then I spent the remaining £600 on a two-week holiday in Ireland. I took the whole family, eight of us, including my grandmother. We stayed in a hotel at Port Marnock near the golf course. I kept spending till the money ran out. I couldn't get rid of it quick enough ...

Chapter Six

In sunny Watford, there was of course great rejoicing, when the lad done good. The local papers had lots of stories in the lead-up to the 1967 Cup Final, about ex-Leggatt's Way Secondary Modern Schoolboy, who still lived with his mum in Watford, appearing in the Cup Final. But the biggest celebrations took place in the Kinnear household. It helped make up for the awful disappointment Joe, and his mother, had suffered when he'd first set out to be a footballer.

'He's had many disappointments on his rocky road,' says Greta, 'but that was the worst. I told him he would succeed, that he would make a great footballer. I told him his father had played for Shamrock Rovers. That was news to him – as I'd never talked about his real father. But I think it impressed him, gave him hope.

'Some time after he'd had that reject letter, there was a knock at the door one morning. It was a Sunday morning, and I was getting ready to go to Mass. They said you won't know who we are and I said oh yes I do, I know exactly who you are. You're from Watford, the club who rejected my son. He only got ten minutes at his trial, what good was that, how you could tell anything about him in ten minutes. I asked them what they were doing on my doorstep. They said they wanted him to join Watford. I said too late. And I shut the door in their faces.'

'When Spurs offered him professional forms, I did say take it, it's what you always wanted, but I then had to go to his work and see the union. I got him his apprenticeship in the first place. It wasn't through Gerry. He worked elsewhere. Someone had told me there was a vacancy at Witherby's, so I went down personally and enquired. I got all the details and arranged the interview for Joe.

'That's why they put me through it, when Joe told them he was now leaving his apprenticeship to be a footballer. They said Joe just couldn't leave. I said but he's signed for Spurs. So he is leaving. They said that's all very well, Mrs Kinnear, but he's already signed his indentures. He has deprived some other boy of a chance. It wouldn't be right, if he now backs out. I said too bad. He's going to be a footballer. They said he's being very foolish.

'Oh, they were just a bunch of forgetmenots. I had no time for them. I think they were hoping to get money out of me, to pay off Joe's indentures. In those days, you often did have to pay. But I wasn't having any of that. I was a fighting 69th. Don't you know that expression? It's Irish, I suppose. My mother used to say it about me. "There she goes, the fighting 69th." It must have been some regiment in some war who didn't stop fighting. That's me, always has been.

'So when Joe started to do well, and got in the first team, I was so pleased for him – it made people eat their words, the ones who had turned him down or not rated him, like Tommy Docherty. I'll never forget someone in one interview saying that my Joe was "average". I still haven't forgiven him. I was hopping. Desmond Hackett in the *Express* said he would eat his hat if Spurs won. I did enjoy the picture on Monday with his hat stuck down his throat.

'Joe won the FA Cup Final on his own. Oh yes. It was all thanks to him. All right, then, why do you think he was Man of the Match?

 Why mum is to miss the match

SHE CAN'T BEAR TO WATCH JOE PLAY

By Pamela Foster-Williams

There will be no prouder Mum on Cup Final Saturday than Mrs. Greta Kinnear, aged 42, of Watford.

No one more anxious, more

"Talking to customers takes my mind off the match. I'm too nervous to go and watch it."

Only once has she seen him play. It was four years ago. It made her ill.

It is not that she doubts the six-footer's ability to take care of himself, and she did not

mean a new streamlined kitchen from her son.

For the family—father. Shirley 23, Carmen 22, Louise 13, Amelia 11 — it will mean a superb holiday.

And where more natural to go than Eire, which Joe left when he was seven. And for whom he won his first cap in February. Turkey

1967: Joe and his mother Greta.

'No, I wasn't there. I never went to watch him play at Spurs. I don't know why. I suppose it's like having a little child in the school play. You don't want to turn up and watch, in case it makes him nervous and he forgets his lines. I thought if I went to watch him at Spurs, I might make him nervous.

'He gave me two tickets for the Cup Final – but I gave them to the sons of the man who owned the fruit and veg stall where I worked. Oh I did that job for many years, in Market Street,

Watford. I always worked on Tuesdays, Friday and Saturdays.

'On Cup Final Saturday, I went to work on the stall as usual. Saturday was our busiest day. But early in the morning, before I got started, I went to the little Catholic church nearby, Holyrood RC Church, yes, like Holyrood Palace. I lit my candle and had a little chat with the Boss Upstairs. I knew then that Joe was going to be the best player on the field. I had no worries, no nerves, not after I'd spoken to the Boss.

'I came back to the stall, and was working there all day. The man in charge, the one I'd given the tickets to, had got hold of a little black and white television. He put it under the stall, so I could watch it from time to time, hear progress, know how Joe was getting on. I saw the beginning, with Joe coming out at Wembley, and I shouted at him, "You're not on your own Joe!" I knew he would do well.

'At the end of the match, Joe was interviewed. He wasn't quite used to this, so you could hear him saying to the interviewer, "Am I on TV?" When the interviewer said yes, Joe said, "I hope you're proud of me, Mum!" Oh, I had a tear in my eye ...

'I tell a lie. I did twice go and watch him play at Spurs. I can't remember which match, but it was at White Hart Lane. I was sat there, surrounded by Herberts. One of them started passing nasty remarks about Joe, how he was useless and he wanted someone else in the team. He was using very foul language. I stood up and hit him with my handbag, gave him three wallops. "Keep your big mouth shut," I screamed at him. "You don't know who's sitting here." Then I stormed out. A policeman or security person stopped me and said I couldn't leave. The gates were shut. The match isn't finished, madam, he said. It is for me, I said. I'm not going to sit there and have people insulting my son. Who's your son, madam? I told him and he said, okay, then. He let me out and I went straight home.

'The second time was much later, a big match, against Wolves I think. Some European final? I'd said I wasn't going, and he'd got rid of the tickets. It was only at the last minute I decided I would go, after he'd badgered me again. So he had to buy a ticket from a tout – which turned out to be at the Wolves end. When Joe tackled a Wolves player, they all started booing him. Everyone round me was booing Joe, so I stood up and gave one of them a wallop. I then sat down and just said nothing. I wasn't walloped back. They just thought it's a little woman, in amongst all these big Wolves supporters. But I did give a big cheer when Spurs won.

'I never went again. That was it. Just two matches, all the time Joe was at Spurs. It was more than enough, thank you. I couldn't stand it ...'

Chapter Seven

What was remarkable about that Spurs Cup Final team of 1967 was what it cost. Pat Jennings was £27,000 from Watford, Cyril Knowles £42,000 from Middlesbrough, Mullery £72,000 from Fulham, Venables £80,000 from Chelsea, England £95,000 from Blackburn, Mackay £28,000 from Hearts, Gilzean £72,500 from Dundee, Robertson £30,000 from St Mirren, Greaves £99,900 from Milan. There were only two players not bought – me and Frank Saul. The total was £564,900. I suppose it seemed a lot at the time – but not now. Imagine a Cup-winning team costing half a million today.

Frank Saul also started as an amateur player, in the youth team, then signed as a professional. As the only free players in the team, we always felt a bit vulnerable, that Bill might go out and buy a replacement for us, if we lost form or got injured.

There had been a rumour that Bill was interested in Jimmy Armfield, captain of Blackpool, who was a right back. He wanted him for my place. Then there were lots of rumours that he was after some Scotsman. Bill loved Scots, as he'd done so well with Dave Mackay, John White, Jimmy Robertson, Bill Brown and then Gilly.

All of the team were established internationals as well. Before I started playing for Ireland, when they were away with their respective countries, me and Frank would be left to train with the reserves. It made you feel out of things. Before the Cup Final, I remember discussing it with Frank, that we would be for the chop, if things went wrong. But of course they didn't. Frank got a goal and I was Man of the Match. That Cup Final win did make me feel a lot better, more secure, more confident. It put me on the map.

In 1967, I also became an international. Our good Cup run had probably helped me when I got called up for the first time in February 1967 for the Republic of Ireland against Turkey in the European Nations Cup.

Ireland had some good full backs at the time – Tony Dunne and Shay Brennan both played for Manchester United and Ireland. The manager was John Carey, who'd also been full back for Manchester United. Then there was Noel Cantwell and Charlie Hurley, both top-class defenders.

I didn't expect to play, being younger and less experienced than any of them. But the manager decided to make a tactical change – he made Noel Cantwell centre forward. He was a six-foot-two centre half, but often in those days a centre half would be sent up as centre forward for the last 15 minutes, if you were losing. This time he was made centre forward for the whole match. So I was brought in as right back. John Giles was captain. Eamonn Dunphy was also playing in midfield that day. The match was away, in Ankara. We got beaten 2-1. But we won 3-0 when we played the return match at home.

In the next two seasons, I played about seven more matches for Ireland. I should have had a lot more caps than I did. It was so badly organized in those days. Spurs had so many European matches at the time, often in the same week as internationals. They didn't space them out. Bill Nick would let me choose what I'd do if there was a clash – playing for Ireland or Spurs. I usually chose Spurs. Despite being a regular at last, I was still a bit worried about losing my place. I hated being put in that position as I loved playing for my country.

I wasn't attacked for doing that by the Irish media, which might happen today. Nobody seemed to care very much. And it did give a chance for local players, those playing for Shamrock Rovers or whatever, to have a game in the national team. It was seen as good PR.

It was only when Johnny Giles took over as the national manager, then it changed. He stopped all that, got properly organized and insisted on any players picked having to turn up. He was very bullish, and quite right too. That's what you should do.

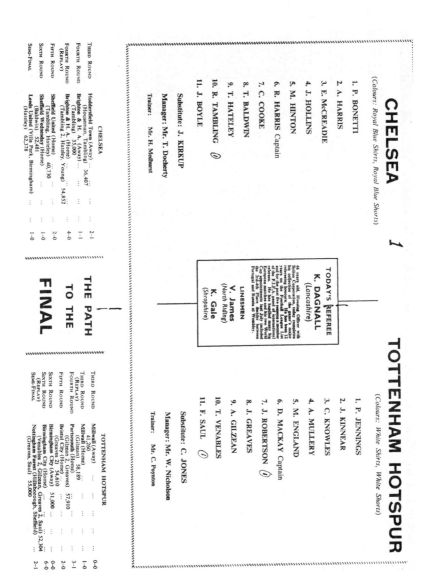

CHELSEA 1   **TOTTENHAM HOTSPUR**

(Colours: Royal Blue Shirts, Royal Blue Shorts)   (Colours: White Shirts, White Shorts)

CHELSEA	TOTTENHAM HOTSPUR
1. P. BONETTI	1. P. JENNINGS
2. A. HARRIS	2. J. KINNEAR
3. E. McCREADIE	3. C. KNOWLES
4. J. HOLLINS	4. A. MULLERY
5. M. HINTON	5. M. ENGLAND
6. R. HARRIS Captain	6. D. MACKAY Captain
7. C. COOKE	7. J. ROBERTSON
8. T. BALDWIN	8. J. GREAVES
9. T. HATELEY	9. A. GILZEAN
10. R. TAMBLING	10. T. VENABLES
11. J. BOYLE	11. F. SAUL

Substitute: J. KIRKUP   Substitute: C. JONES

Manager: Mr. T. Docherty   Manager: Mr. W. Nicholson

Trainer: Mr. H. Medhurst   Trainer: Mr. C. Poynton

TODAY'S REFEREE

K. DAGNALL

(Lancashire)

46 years old, Housing Officer with Bolton Corporation, today completes his collection of the game's major refereeing honours. He has been 12 years on the Football League List and for the past five seasons a member of the F.I.F.A. panel of international referees. He has handled many big European matches and his two World Cup appointments last July included the 3rd-4th Place decider between Portugal and Russia at Wembley.

LINESMEN

V. James
(North Riding)

K. Gale
(Shropshire)

THE PATH TO THE FINAL

	CHELSEA			TOTTENHAM HOTSPUR		
THIRD ROUND	Huddersfield Town (Away) (Houseman, Tambling)	36,407	2-1	Millwall (Away)	41,260	0-0
FOURTH ROUND	Brighton & H. A. (Away) (Tambling)	35,000	1-1	Millwall (Home) (Gilzean)	58,189	1-0
(REPLAY)						
FOURTH ROUND	Brighton & H. A. (Home) (Tambling 2, Hateley, Young)	54,852	4-0	Portsmouth (Home)	57,910	3-1
(REPLAY)						
FIFTH ROUND	Sheffield United (Home) (Tambling, Hateley)		2-0	Bristol City (Home) (Greaves 2)	54,610	2-0
SIXTH ROUND	Sheffield Wednesday (Home)	40,730	1-0	Birmingham City (Away) (Greaves 2)	51,000	0-0
SEMI-FINAL	Leeds United (Villa Park, Birmingham) (Hateley)	62,378	1-0	Birmingham City (Home) (Venables 2, Gilzean, Greaves 2, Saul)	52,304	6-0
				Nottingham Forest (Hillsborough, Sheffield) (Greaves, Saul)	55,000	2-1

Cup Final Programme, 1967.

42

TOTTENHAM HOTSPUR

PAT JENNINGS, *Goalkeeper*

Regular Northern Ireland international with 15 caps. Cost £30,000 from Watford in June, 1964. Born Newry, Co. Down. Assessor of the largest pair of hands in football. Brilliant cup consistency this season. Aged 22. Height 6 ft. Weight 12 st.

JOE KINNEAR, *Right Back*

A year ago had not even made League debut. Dublin-born Joe (middle name Patrick, of course!) is small, clever ball player, capped once for Eire. Models his style on Danny Blanchflower. A £20 signing in this £625,000 Spurs team. Aged 20. Height 5 ft. 7 ins. Weight 10 st. 10 lb.

CYRIL KNOWLES, *Left Back*

Yorkshire-born. Had short spells with Manchester United and Wolves as youngster. Signed in May, 1964, from Middlesbrough for £45,000. England Under-23 international. Fast, swift-tackling, superb team man. Married his childhood sweetheart this year. Aged 23. Height 6 ft. Weight 11 st. 8 lb.

ALAN MULLERY, *Right Half*

London-born, former Fulham star. Cost £72,500 when signed in March, 1964. England international. Missed 1964 Brazil tour with England because he picked his back cleaning his teeth. A manager's ideal player. Flawless in the semi-final victory over Forest. Aged 25. Height 5 ft. 8½ ins. Weight 12 st. 8 lb.

MIKE ENGLAND, *Centre Half*

Regarded by many as Britain's best centre half. Transferred from Blackburn Rovers at season's start for £95,000. Regular Welsh No. 5 with 22 caps. Prestatyn-born. Clever, versatile, commanding. Another semi-final hero. Aged 26. Height 6 ft. 1 in. Weight 13 st. 1 lb.

DAVE MACKAY, *Left Half (Captain)*

One of three survivors from the 1962 Cup-winning Spurs team. Has broken his leg twice since then. Inspiring captain, Scottish international with 22 caps, cost £30,000 when signed from Hearts eight years ago. Played at Wembley in last three internationals. Aged 30. Height 5 ft. 8 ins. Weight 11 st. 2 lb. Scottish schoolboy hero.

JIMMY ROBERTSON, *Outside Right*

Another Scottish international. Transferred from St. Mirren in March, 1964, for £23,000. Spent a few months on the Middlesbrough ground staff. Tricky, fast, goal-conscious. Plays on either wing. A Scottish youth and Under-23 international. Aged 25. Height 5 ft. 8 in. Weight 10 st.

JIMMY GREAVES, *Inside Right*

The man who has played for both Cup Finalists today. Goal king of English football. Cost Spurs £99,999 from Milan in November, 1961, just in time to win a 1962 Cup medal. Has played 55 times and scored 43 goals for England. Netted 102 goals in last three Chelsea seasons. Top scorer for Spurs in the past five seasons. Aged 27. Height 5 ft. 8 in. Weight 10 st. 9 lb.

ALAN GILZEAN, *Centre Forward*

Third Scottish international (10 caps) in the side. Tall, graceful, ball artist. Signed for £72,500 from Dundee in December, 1964. Perth-born although playing first at senior level with Aldershot. Links adroitly with Greaves in Spurs' G-man attack. Aged 27. Height 5 ft. 10 in. Weight 12 st.

TERRY VENABLES, *Inside Left*

Yet another who has played for both finalists. Transferred from Chelsea in May last year for £80,000. England international. Dagenham-born. A man who has represented his country at schoolboy, amateur and Under-23 level. Aged 24. Height 5 ft. 8 in. Weight 10 st. 12 lb.

FRANK SAUL, *Outside Left*

Only uncapped member of the side. Cost Spurs £20 when signed on professionally in 1960. Never really established a regular spot in the side. Scorer of the decisive second goal at Sheffield in the semi-final. Born Canvey Island. Aged 24. Height 5 ft. 10 in. Weight 11 st. 10 lb.

CLIFF JONES

Swansea-born, a famous Welsh international (54 caps) of flying wing fame. Injury plagued this season. Like Mackay and Greaves a 1962 Cup medal winner with Spurs. Father of four. A butcher by trade. Played in more than 300 League matches with Spurs. Aged 32. Height 5 ft. 6½ in. Weight 10 st. 8 lb.

JIMMY GREAVES ON GOAL TARGET!

(Picture by Evening Standard)

No wonder the Forest defenders look anxious! It's the one and only Jimmy Greaves in goal-hungry mood during the F.A. Cup semi-final tie at Hillsborough. Greaves failed to find the net on this occasion but he put Spurs on the road to Wembley with a wonderful goal in the 32nd minute.

● **SAM LEITCH** *(Contd. from page 15)*

There is a natural tendency for the entire football world to shriek acclaim for the twenty-two footballers on the field this afternoon.

Spare a considerable thought for the patient, far-seeing, highly practical Nicholson as he leads his men out. Nicholson is the man who has played, coached and managed Spurs history for three decades.

A mention also for the back-room boys of White Hart Lane. Pipe-smoking Eddie Baily, Nick's right hand, and that incredible character of a trainer, Cecil Poynton, himself a playing stalwart of Spurs in the middle and late 20's. Finally secretary Reg Jarvis, 12 years devoted service to Spurs behind him.

These are the line men who make Tottenham tick. Hotspur the club founded under a lamp post in Tottenham High Street. Spurs—a five-letter word which spells out Sophistication, Persistence, Urgency, Reputation and Success.

JOE WAS CUP FINAL STAR

"I WOULD single out our right back—he had an exceptional game." So said Spurs' Manager Bill Nicholson about the lad who cost a mere £20 signing on fee and who outshadowed many of the stars on parade at the FA Cup Final on Saturday.

That right back is Joe Kinnear, who lives in Queen's Road, Watford, and is a former pupil of Leggatts Way School. . . . And what a glorious game Joe played for victorious Spurs. His instructions were to shadow Bobby Tambling, but as he told the "Observer," Tambling was playing so far back and with Eddie McCreadie following Jimmy Robertson away from the right there was acres of space for me to attack down the right."

Twice Joe teed up gilt-edged chances for his colleagues by cutting in from the right flank. Joe was only worried once during the match when the wandering Tambling redeemed a goal for Chelsea. "I thought there were just a couple of minutes to go but when that goal came about six minutes were left and they seemed like an age."

Nevertheless, the medal which Joe cherishes even more than his Eire international cap was safe and the celebrations bubbled until the early hours of Sunday morning.

Right now Joe is packing for a tour to Switzerland with Spurs, who have arranged three friendly matches there. This will be yet another country added to the list of America, Canada, Bermuda, Mexico, Germany, Poland and Turkey which he has visited on his football travels.

Joe was not the first Watford winner of an FA Cup-winners' medal. In 1921 that great Spurs and England captain Arthur Grimsdell was in the Tottenham team which defeated Wolverhampton Wanderers 1-0, and in the Wolves' team was Eddie Edmonds, who, like Grimsdell, went to Watford Field School.

1967: Cup Final praise from Bill Nick.

Something I'll never forget happened after one of my early games for Ireland, during that first season playing for them. It was a home game against Czechoslovakia, held at Daleymount Park in Dublin. I was running off the pitch after the game, heading for the dressing room, when I could hear a voice shouting, 'Joe, Joe, Joe!' It took me a few seconds to realize who it was. Then I went over to speak to him.

'I'm your father,' he said. I said, 'I know.' I hadn't actually seen him since I was about six. I was then 20. I said I had to go to the dressing room now, but he should come round to the players' entrance. I'd meet him there, after I'd got dressed, then we'd go and have a drink.

I had nothing against him personally. My mother had never told me what happened. She'd kept it back, whatever had gone wrong. All I knew was that the marriage hadn't worked. But I felt no resentment towards him. Anyway, I waited and waited outside the players' entrance. But he never came. So I gave up.

Some of my aunts told me later that he was choked that he hadn't been a good father, embarrassed by what had happened. After he'd spoken to me, he'd apparently had a change of heart, deciding it was better not to see me again.

I'd never clapped eyes on him all those years, since I'd left Dublin, but he had worked out who Joe Kinnear was. He realized I was really Joe Reddy, his son, which nobody else knew. It had never come out. He was obviously very proud of what I'd done, playing for Spurs and Ireland. I think he'd even made several trips to London to watch me play for Spurs. That's what I was told later. I never knew, because he never tried to make contact with me.

I never spoke to him again, and didn't see him again, except for the day he was dying. This was a few years later on his death bed. My mother was called to Dublin: he'd had a heart attack, in his early 50s. He was too far gone when I arrived. A shame, really: I would have liked to have heard his full story, of what happened. And I'm sure he would have liked to have been in touch with me, when I started coming through into the Spurs team, sharing things like the Cup Final triumph and my success generally, especially when I had a few bob in my pocket. I could have helped him a bit.

PLAYED FOR EIRE

Pictured in the Eire shirt he wore when he made his international debut against Turkey on Wednesday of last week is Spurs' full-back Joe Kinnear, who lives in Watford and is an old boy of Leggatts Way School. Joe played at right back in Ankara and will be in line for selection again when Eire play Czechoslovakia at the end of the season. Although born in Dublin, Joe has spent most of his life in Watford.

THE best of the legion of stories about Joe Kinnear is the one that is **not** true.

It is said that when he was first selected for the Irish team, for a match against Turkey in Ankara in 1967, the band played the long version of the national anthem, "seo dhaoibh a chairde," agus ar lean.

Joe is reported to have turned to his colleague in the line and said: "I hope our one is not that long."

Providing he survived last night's stag party in Cork for Wimbledon player Vinny Jones, Joe Kinnear will sit with John Giles in judgement of our World Cup adventure over the coming four weeks.

His idea of compensating for his strange accent is to adopt an entirely partisan approach to his analysis, using "we" and "us" freely in a way that would not be expected or indeed appropriate for Eamon Dunphy.

'CAP' FOR KINNEAR

JOE KINNEAR, the Watford boy who plays for Spurs, gained his first international cap when he played for Eire against Turkey at Ankara on Wednesday afternoon.

Although Eire were beaten 2-1 on a very difficult playing surface, Kinnear gave an excellent account of himself and staked a strong claim for a place in the Eire side which meets Czechoslovakia in May at Dublin.

Joe, who was born in Ireland but has lived nearly all his life in Watford, is a former Watford Schoolboy representative player and has been with Spurs for three seasons.

He said after returning from Turkey last night: "It was a wonderful experience. I thoroughly enjoyed it."

His selection came as a reward for determination and dedication in a season in which his football has provided a battle against injury.

Some stories about Joe's Irish games.

Chapter Eight

Being at Spurs in the late 60s and early 70s, in a so-called glamour team, we did have lots of girls hanging around us. Nothing like today, though at the time there seemed to be a lot. As the team's bachelor, I did get many fan letters and marriage offers, probably about 50 letters a week. Today, David Beckham probably has 500 a week.

A lot of girls were just young tarts but some were older women, wives of middle-aged North London dress manufacturers whose husbands were away a lot on business. They used to organize little parties and invite Spurs players, show them little films. They were very keen on young, fit, athletic types ...

We also got invited up West a lot, to charity dinners and functions in Mayfair, boxing matches, galas and stuff. I was hardly out of my dinner jacket at the time.

Contacts between the world of show business and football were just beginning, so you'd rub shoulders with famous pop stars, people in groups, television stars. I don't think this had really happened much before, with the Double team of 1961, for instance. It came in a bit later, towards the end of the sixties.

After training, I'd often go up West with Terry Venables to Tin Pan Alley. We'd go and have a drink in one of the show-biz offices, meet people like the Moody Blues. I can remember Elton John as a tea-boy, loading sheet music into vans.

I met Eric Hall at that time. He was in the music business, not a football agent. It was through him that I met a pop star called Tina

Charles. People don't remember her now, but she had a No. 1 hit with 'I Loved to Love'. Eric put around this story that we were inseparable, that we were going to get married. When I got injured, he arranged for her to visit me – with photographers in tow. It was a complete set-up. I hardly knew her.

Terry and I would then move on from Tin Pan Alley to other showbiz hang-outs, then in the evening we'd end up at one of their parties. I just trailed along after Venables. He was amazing, larger than life. I'd never met anyone like him.

I met the Dave Clark Five, who were top of the charts with 'Bits and Pieces'. They were playing at the Tottenham Royal and for a publicity picture, they all wore Spurs strips. Common stunt now, but very unusual then.

You didn't need to spend much, as everything was free. People were always giving you things, which meant I managed to save quite a bit, especially as I was still living at home with my mum in Watford.

I bought myself a sports car, an MGB GT, and then I invested in two houses in Watford, in the same street as my mother's. I paid £1,800 for each of them, getting a mortgage, then converted them into flats. I let them out and collected the rent myself. One of my first tenants was a single guy, a drummer in a band. When he finished in the band, which was going nowhere, he went into insurance. Now he's got houses and helicopters, everything, and is worth millions. I still see him from time to time.

But I got into tax trouble with the rents. I'd had some advice from some so-called business expert when I'd bought the flats, but it was rubbish. I got investigated by the tax people. I'd been collecting the rents in cash and not declaring. All I'd done with the money was pay the bills, pay for the conversion and pay the mortgage on the houses. I thought you could do that. I wasn't prosecuted or anything. They just found out and said I had to pay up all the tax I hadn't paid. Which I did. I think it was about £3,000. Seemed a lot at the time, but nothing now.

When my Spurs contract was coming up in 1968, I decided to ask for a lot more, as we'd won the Cup by then. It was the first time I'd ever thought of doing so. But I wasn't really brave enough to face

Bill Nick on my own, so I decided to go in and see him with Jimmy Robertson. We discussed beforehand what we were going to say, what we would demand.

When we got into Bill's office, we sat there side by side, in front of his desk. He was reading some documents, which made us both very nervous. He eventually says yes, he's going to offer us both a new two-year contract. He hands us a sheet each, inside a folder, which we both look at and try to understand. There were no agents in those days, no lawyers to help you. A player was just on his own, trying to work out what the language meant. And no player I knew of ever thought of asking them to throw in extra perks, a clothes allowance, new carpets, a travel allowance, a car, an extra car for the wife, none of the ludicrous perks that agents get written into players' contracts today.

So we sat looking at our sheets, puzzling out the words. Bill says, 'Yes, any problems?' We both froze. Neither knew what to say, despite all the things we'd agreed to demand. In turn we said, 'Yeah, that sounds all right to me,' then we stood up and walked out. A complete couple of chickens. Once we got outside, we asked each other what we'd got. We got exactly the same, in the same words. I think there was a small rise, taking us up to about £40 a week.

Whenever I meet players of my generation today, one of the first things we all say to each other is – were we all mugs! How come we earned so little? We had huge crowds of 50,000, yet earned so little. Where did it all go? Bill himself had earned very little. He was always telling us what a wonderful life we had: just think of people struggling down the pits. He said we were lucky – and we believed him.

When Dave Mackay left Spurs in July 1968, to go to Derby, Alan Mullery took over as captain. He was never as popular as Dave, but then Dave was an exceptional person. Mullers was forceful on the pitch, but he didn't socialize much with the lads. He went home after training to his wife.

There was no players' lounge at White Hart Lane in those days – but no player went straight home after a game. We didn't allow it. You didn't want anyone who'd perhaps had a bad game going home feeling miserable. I did the same at Wimbledon. I told Vinnie Jones to make sure no one went straight home, whatever happened in the match. I think that's vital.

What happened at Spurs in the sixties and seventies was that we went to one of two pubs in the High Road – either the Bell and Hare or the Corner Pin. They're both still there. We had a private room, at the back, which was kept for us. The public couldn't get in. We'd stay there for about two hours after every home game. No wives, no friends, just the players: mates, chilling out, relaxing together, after work.

Gradually people would go over every incident. If you'd played a terrible back-pass, you'd talk it through. If you'd had a stinker, you'd end up accepting it, then cry on someone's shoulder. The others would try to cheer you up.

What happens if you go straight home after a bad game is that you just mope. You arrive home with the hump, turn into a really stupid bastard, then take it out on the wife or kids. After our two hours of chilling out and chatting, we'd say cheerio, have a good weekend. Then we'd go home, to our own families. It wasn't a drinking session, though we'd knock back a few pints. It was more therapy.

In many clubs today, that doesn't happen. Some don't even go to the players' lounge. They are off with their agent, or sponsor, or whatever. They don't get the game out of their system.

In the season after the Cup win, '67-68, I played in most games, 37 league and Cup appearances in all. We ended up 7th in the league, which wasn't too bad. But in the next season, on 18 January 1969, I had the worst injury I'd ever had.

It was a home game against Leeds. I think it was Eddie Gray who caught me as I was clearing the ball. It wasn't his fault. He wasn't that type. I had my eyes completely on the ball, and was about to whack it hard, when he came up on my blind side. I always teach defenders to keep an eye on their blind side when they're clearing the ball, in case they get caught. I didn't: I smacked the ball hard with my right foot, just as he arrived. It was my own force which did the damage. So it was wham, bosh, and I went down in absolute agony. My leg sort of forked back onto me. I could feel pools of blood in my boot, sackloads of it. They tried to straighten me out, as I was lying there on the pitch, and I let out more screams of agony. They don't do that today. The theory now is not to touch you, they just slide you onto a stretcher, touching nothing, till you're in hospital.

I'd broken two bones, my fib and my tib. That was it. I was obviously going to be out for months and months, perhaps forever, if it didn't sort itself properly.

For most of the next six months, I was in hospital, at Stanmore Orthopaedic, lying with my leg up in plaster. The worst part is when you itch underneath the plaster, which was from my ankle right up to my thigh. I developed an itching stick, a thin cane which you tie up plants with. I would shove it down the inside of my plaster when it got really hellish itchy.

They put a plate into the leg, where it was broken, with nuts and bolts. Then for four months I was in traction, lying with weights on my leg to build it up.

The lads came to see me once a week. But you still feel so isolated, out of everything, that's the worst part. I worried all the time that Bill would buy someone in my place, but he never did. He just moved Phil Beal back to full back. I'd been lucky when he broke his arm and got his place. Now he was lucky that I'd broken my leg.

And you get so bored. I just read books all the time – Charlie Buchan's Football Monthly, those sort of books. I got so depressed, thinking will I ever play again.

As I got a bit better, they fixed this sort of wheel thing under my right foot, over the plaster, so I could walk around a little bit, with a walking frame or on one crutch, wheeling my right foot. When the plaster eventually came off, my right leg was like a skeleton's. It had withered away so much I'd lost four inches on my calf muscle.

I then spent several months building it up. I went for rehab treatment at White Hart Lane, and I used to walk up and down the stairs in the main stand, till my leg was strong enough to go jogging. Cecil Poynton was in charge of me, but mostly I was totally on my own, getting very lonely.

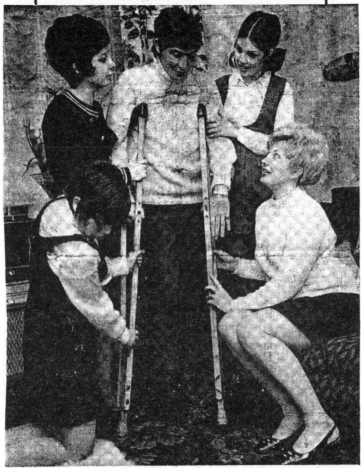

A SOCCER FAMILY'S SUPPORTING CLUB

HE'S GOT a broken leg? He should be so lucky!

Joe Kinnear, Spurs and Ireland full-back, finds convalescence at his home in Watford a bearable trial with four sisters to help his recovery.

If he didn't have the crutches he would still have (clockwise from bottom left) Amelia (14), Shirley (25), Louise (16) and Carmen (24) to lean on.

Kinnear broke his leg at White Hart Lane on January 19 against Leeds. He will not play again this season.

PICTURE BY OWEN BARNES

1969: Joe's worst every injury.

The worst times were Saturdays. Eventually, I was able to go to the ground, and watch matches, so I got a bit of the match-day atmosphere, had a chat with the lads beforehand, a cup of tea, then

I went up into the stand. Sitting watching them play, that was terrible. So near, yet still so far away.

I didn't go in the dressing room before a game. That was sort of sacred. Bill didn't like people doing that. But afterwards, when Bill had left the dressing room, I'd go in and talk to them about the game, then go for a drink with them afterwards.

Altogether, I lost about a year of my football life. I lost the rest of that season and most of the next season, 1969–70, managing only thirteen league games, coming back when I wasn't quite ready. In fact I didn't feel back to proper form and fitness for almost eighteen months. It was a terrible time.

Chapter Nine

It was while Joe was injured that he first met Bonnie Arnold, now his wife, back in 1969.

'I'd gone for a pub lunch with Jimmy Greaves, Dave Mackay and Cliffy Jones at the Old Hall Tavern, Winchmore Hill', said Joe. 'We often used to go there after training. Dave lived just two minutes away at the time.

'Bonnie was at the next table, with a girlfriend, having their lunch, and we somehow got talking to them. I was busy giving her the big 'un, trying to chat her up. "Don't you know who we are?" That sort of style. Anyway, I got talking to her and said why don't you join us at our table. So I brought her over.

'I introduced her to the players I was with. "This is Jimmy Greaves," I said. "This is Dave Mackay, this is Cliff Jones." She sat down and then turned to Jimmy Greaves and said, "And what do you do?" She wasn't putting it on; she was clueless. We all believed the whole world knew who Jimmy Greaves was. She didn't: she had no interest in football, and still knows nothing. Anyway I somehow got her phone number then later rang her up, invited her out for a meal. The Horse and Chains, I think it was, a pub in Bushey. Then it somehow just proceeded from there.'

At that moment, Bonnie came into the room. Joe asked her if she remembered the day they first met, at the Old Hall Tavern.

'No it wasn't,' said Bonnie.

'Oh Gawd, you're not going to deny everything I say? You do remember the occasion though, don't you? I was there with Dave Mackay, Jimmy Greaves and Cliff Jones.'

'Dave Mackay wasn't there,' said Bonnie. 'He'd left Spurs by then. It was Mike England.'

'Well I got two right out of three. Not bad. You do remember me being there as well, don't you?'

'I was with two people actually,' said Bonnie, 'a girlfriend and a male friend. And it was this man who knew someone in Joe's party. In fact I'd seen Joe earlier, through this man, at another social gathering. He was in plaster at the time, after his broken leg. But I didn't talk to him. I just remember this person in plaster.

'I don't like the implication, Joe, that I was picked-up in a pub. Do you mind. We were invited to join Joe's group for lunch because of a mutual friend.'

'Yeah, but I then got your phone number, didn't I?'

'I don't know how. What I remember was you putting your hand on my knee?'

'Did I? Leave orf ...'

'Oh you did.'

'Well you was probably wearing a mini-skirt and leather boots. You was asking for it,' said Joe, giving a big dirty laugh.

'My first impression of Joe was that he was one of the most obnoxious people I'd ever met ...'

'Thanks a bunch,' said Joe.

Joe had no regular girlfriend at the time. There had been a girl called Carol he'd gone out with for some years. She had been at school with him in Watford and he had taken her to Spurs' 1967 Cup Final party. But that had finished.

'What I had was a bookload of girls. On Monday, I'd get out my book and think now, who should I take out? Then next day I'd ring another one. They were just dates, one night stands, nothing serious.

'I was the only bachelor in the Spurs team, so I always appeared to have more girlfriends than I really had. I became the alibi for everyone else. If they got spotted by someone in a pub with a girlfriend, and there were lots of bizzies, even in those days, then the players would say oh, not me, she wasn't with me, that's all wrong, she was Joe's girl. I would go along with it, back them up. They could always say they were going out with me, if they were going where they shouldn't be going.

'There were girls who rang the club, threatening to expose some player, unless they got paid. The player would get called in and deny it, saying it had been Joe, not them. Didn't matter to me. As a single bloke, I had nothing to lose.'

Bonnie was in a mini-skirt that first day they met properly, and leather boots – this was the sixties. She was blonde, attractive, well spoken, very lively. What Joe didn't know about her was that she was running her own business. Or that she was married, with two children.

Bonnie was born and brought up in North London, an only child. Her father was in the fashion business. She went to private schools and then a secretarial college. She had only been working for a year when she got married.

'I was very young.' How old? 'About thirteen. Let's say too young anyway. After a couple of years, I knew it was a mistake.'

By that time she had a little boy, Elliot, and a baby girl, Russelle. 'I had separated when I met Joe, about to get divorced. I told him all this. Made no secret of it.'

The business she was running was a trendy unisex clothes shop called Fella in the middle of Hampstead Village – Heath Street, opposite the Tube station. I can clearly remember Bonnie as being very bright and sparky.

'I enjoyed having the shop. I ran it for about three years, but then the lease came up. The main owner, as I remember it, was supposed to be Cynthia Lennon. One of the Beatles' companies had invested in various buildings in Heath Street. The new rent was going to be enormous, so I gave it up. I had my children to look after, though I did have a live-in nanny. Then of course meeting Joe. That did rather change things ...'

'When I found out about Bonnie's background,' said Joe,

'about her divorce, and being Jewish, it never bothered me. Me and Bonnie just seemed to gel, right from the beginning. It quickly became a love job.

'I knew it might bother my mother, so it was a while before I took her home. I was of course still living at home. I also worried about her two kids. How would they take their mother having a boyfriend? But I thought well, let it run its course, let it work itself out ...'

After about a year of going out, they decided to live together, with Joe moving into Bonnie's house, then they bought a house, a semi-detached in Woodside Park, Totteridge.

From the very beginning, Joe looked upon her two young children as his own. He has always considered them as such, still referring to them as his children. They call him Dad, as they have always done.

'From the moment I took Bonnie home to meet my mother, it was brilliant. No problems. And I had no problems with her mother. It all worked out well. As far as I know, it was perfectly accepted on either side ...'

'I wouldn't quite go so far as to say that,' said Bonnie. 'I did sense some opposition. There was some stress in the early years. But here we are, thirty years later. We survived it ...

'The biggest stress of all was football, as anyone married to a footballer well knows. You don't marry a player; you marry his profession. It was all an enormous shock to the system. I hadn't known a thing about football, till I met Joe. It took some getting used to.

'I had been used to being independent, with my own business and with my own family life. I had to come to terms with the fact that football would now be greater than any of them. Football came first. On a Saturday morning, when Joe was getting ready for a match, the children were not allowed to make a peep, in case they might disturb the master.

'The club was not interested in any of the players' wives or our problems. That's changed a bit, in recent years. They do consider the home situation, especially if it might affect a player. But in those days, you didn't exist. Bill Nick was not interested in me or my domestic arrangements.

'At home, when Joe was dropped, it was a nightmare. Unbearable. He was impossible to be with. Usually though, as the week went on, he'd pick himself up. He is basically an optimist, but after a bad game, oh God, I dreaded that. Or a serious injury, like the one he had when I first met him.'

What about, er, the girls, the ones whom I saw even then, back in the early seventies? That must have been hard to get used to.

'Going out with Joe to a public place, a pub or a restaurant, or to a party, girls would literally push me out of the way. They'd shove me aside, as if I didn't exist, to get at Joe. I was so shocked. It's much worse today, but even then, there were girls throwing themselves at footballers.

'You have to accept that, as a wife or a girlfriend. It's part of the territory. If you can't accept it, then get out. Then when they travel away, you have to accept that as well, what might happen. It's no different with rugby players, golfers, or businessmen when they go away. We know what boys can get up to. All you hope is not to be publicly humiliated. What you need is a good basic relationship. And to be a realist. I knew that Joe was a charmer.

'It wasn't of course as blatant as it is today, or as public. Wives could easily be completely unaware. I think it was partly because a lot of the press who followed the teams were up to the same things, so they didn't write about it. Now it gets written about all the time. Girls rush to sell their little tacky stories for thousands of pounds. It's the girls who are so blatant today. Shocking, really.

'I managed to survive all that better than most of the wives and girlfriends, being a bit older than some of them, having been married already. That helped. It's the very young wives who suffer most, then and now, stuck at home with very young babies, often in a strange city, in a strange culture. I was born and brought up in North London. I knew about the sort of social life Joe was having. I didn't feel out of it, going to the theatre, dinners, parties, meeting celebrities. When football marriages collapse, it's often because the young wife can't cope. She feels out of it and becomes resentful of the pressures she's put under.'

Chapter Ten

After I came back from my leg injury, I became a regular again in the Spurs team. In 1971, we got to the League Cup Final. We beat Aston Villa, 2-0, with Martin Chivers scoring both goals. Then two years later we got to the final again, this time playing Norwich. We beat them 1-0. What I clearly remember about that game was John Pratt getting injured then Ralph Coates came on in his place – and scored.

Ralph's nickname in the dressing room was 'Swoop' because of his hair. He swooped it back across his head to cover his baldness, the way Bobby Charlton used to do. Cyril Knowles used to take the piss out of Ralph something rotten really, but we all went along with it, as you do in a dressing room, when someone gets wound up. Cyril used to maintain that Ralph combed his hair from under his armpit, in order to get it onto his head.

Me and Cyril once planned to capture Ralph. We were going to grab him after training, tie him down, then cut off all his hair, such as it was, even the wispy bits, leaving him totally bald. We never did it, chickened out. At Wimbledon, if some of the lads had decided on such a trick, nothing would have stopped them.

The Spurs fans used to shout 'Nice One Cyril' at Cyril Knowles, which became a pop song of the time. The song they used to sing for me was 'In Dublin's fair city, where the girls are so pretty, I first set my eye upon sweet Joey Kinnear. As he wheels his wheelbarrow, through streets broad and narrow, crying – TOTTING-HAM! Totting-HAM! TOTTING-HAM!'

WINNERS OF THE "DOUBLE" F.A CUP AND LEAGUE CHAMPIONSHIP 1960 61. AND "THE EUROPEAN CUP WINNERS CUP" 1962 3

TELEPHONE: TOTTENHAM 1020   TELEGRAMS: SPURS LOWER TOTTENHAM

TOTTENHAM HOTSPUR FOOTBALL & ATHLETIC CO. LTD.

MEMBERS OF THE FOOTBALL ASSOCIATION AND THE FOOTBALL LEAGUE

| LEAGUE CHAMPIONS
1951   1961
SECRETARY: G W. JONES | 748 HIGH ROAD
TOTTENHAM · N.17
CHAIRMAN FRED. WALE | WINNERS OF F.A CUP
1901, 1921, 1961, 1962,
1967
MANAGER: W. E. NICHOLSON |

9. 5. 70.

Dear Joe,

                    Tottenham Hotspur Football Club
                    Offer of Further Re-Engagement.

        In accordance with the terms of Clause 18(b) of the
Agreement made the   5th. August 1968   between the above Club
and yourself, I, as Secretary acting with the authority and on
behalf of such Club, now give you Notice that the Club hereby
offers you a further re-engagement for a period of one year
from the 30th day of June next, on the following terms:-

(1)   The provisions of the present Agreement shall be
           incorporated in a new written Agreement to be entered
           into between you and the Club for the proposed period
           of   one year   from the 30th day of June next.

(2)   Your remuneration during the proposed period to be:

           £70 per week basic wage.
           £10 for each first team appearance.
           £5 being a further payment for each first team appearance.

(3)   In addition to the above basic wages you would be paid:

           As set out in section 15. Other Financial Provisions.

        I shall be obliged if you will reply to me as soon as
possible, and I enclose a stamped addressed envelope for your use.

                    Yours faithfully,

                    Secretary. Tottenham Hotspur F.C.

*A period piece: from a time when star players at a star club
managed on non-starry wages.*

*Martin Peters was admired by everyone. It was his ability off the
ball which made him so brilliant, able to pop up out of nowhere and
score so many vital goals from midfield. He was a master at timing*

his runs and losing his marker. I always thought Martin would have made a great career for himself in management.

Jimmy Greaves never had to work at his game – he was just so talented. In training, all he mainly did was practise goal scoring. It was amazing to watch him. Apart from that, he didn't like training and hated stuff like running or cross-country. When we had to do it, he would beg lifts on milk-floats, or hide a bike and ride it home. If he was forced to do the whole run, because Eddie Bailey or some-one was watching his every step, he'd come in half an hour after most of us had gone home. If he still hadn't appeared, one of the lads would go and pick him up in his car.

Martin Chivers could be brilliant – and he won the UEFA Cup Final for us in 1972 with his two away goals in the first leg at Wolves. But he and Bill Nick didn't always get on, or understand each other. I used to room with Martin. When he had problems with his first wife and they were splitting up, he came to live with me for a few weeks. It was through me he met his second wife. I took him to Walthamstow dog track one evening, and he met his new wife there. She was related to one of the owners. They've been very happy ever since and running their pub business together.

(I remember once, a few years later, meeting a lad called David Beckham at Walthamstow dogs. He was collecting up the dirty glasses. Must have been about 15 at the time, doing an evening job. Someone told me he wanted to be a footballer. I wonder what happened to him?)

Bill Nick was a great manager. I admired him tremendously and had some great years with him. I played for him in four cup finals – and we won them all. Shows he was doing something right. If he had a fault, it was that he often made out that the opposition was better than they were. Now and again he would frighten the life out of us, making their defenders sound 10 feet tall and their attackers seem better than Pelé. I know now he was just trying to stop us becoming complacent, but I think at times he overdid it.

We also had the Double team hanging over us. He was always on about them, and made us feel a bit inferior, that we would never be up to their level. You rarely got praise out of Bill. Being picked – that *was the most praise you ever got. But his record as a manager was remarkable. He was a perfectionist, who ate, slept and lived for Spurs.*

I met Bill shortly after I went into management and I asked him for any advice on the contract I was being offered. 'Joe, your only security is your ability.' That was really what Bill thought about football, whether you were a player or a manager. And of course, in the end, it's perfectly true.

Chapter Eleven

'We knew our place, as Spurs wives in the 1960s and 1970s,' says Bonnie, 'but we all got on very well together. If someone's husband had replaced another husband in the team, there was no jealousy. We all understood.

'We did have a little tea room in the stand where we all met on match days. Then we all sat together and watched the match. I went to most of the home games, but I didn't really travel.

'You only got invited to anything officially by the club when they got to a cup final. There would then be a special wives' coach, which went to Wembley, some time after the players' coach had gone. Afterwards, you would be invited to the celebration dinner. Apart from that you didn't really exist.

'But one day, Kathy Peters and I decided we would go to an away match, all on our own. When we told Joe and Martin, they were not at all keen. But we said we're going. It was a UEFA Cup match away in Portugal, against Setubal, in March 1973. We just went with the ordinary supporters, travelling there on these six massive coaches. I was late getting to the coaches and Kathy got on one ahead of me. I can still see her, running up and down the aisles, screaming my name in her wonderful cockney accent, trying to find out which coach I'd got on. What a day it was.

'When we got to Lisbon, and checked into our hotel, we went round to the team hotel. We just walked in. You should have seen Bill Nick's face when he saw us. We just ignored him and walked into the hotel lounge. The players were there, sitting around, playing cards. We talked to them for a bit. No touching of course, none of that. Just a few minutes chat, then we went back to our hotel. But we could tell that Joe and Martin were not best pleased at us turning up.

'When we got to the stadium next day, we found there was no segregation, as we had at Spurs. All the rival supporters were mixed up together. A pitched battle soon started. There were bottles flying, knives flashing, people getting cut. "When they find out we've got mixed up in this, the boys will kill us," we said to each other. Spurs won on aggregate, so the Portuguese fans were even more furious.

'After the game, trying to get out, we were getting pretty scared, but some Spurs supporters saved us. They sort of handed us over the crowd and we escaped the worst of the violence. They said don't go back on the coach, that'll be dangerous, so one of them got us a taxi back to the hotel. Just as well: our coach got stoned and all its windows broken. The boys were furious. "Never do that again," they warned us.

'When Spurs went to Feyenoord, for the second leg of the UEFA Cup Final in 1974, that was different. It was a final, so we went officially with the club, and they looked after us. But what was funny was that all those not married were given separate bedrooms. Martin Chivers was not at the time married to Julia and I wasn't married to Joe, so we were allocated separate rooms.'

Joe and Bonnie never had children together. She says the subject never came up. She had two very young children already, whom Joe looked upon as his own, and that seemed enough for both of them.

Once they got a bit older, Bonnie decided to go back to work. She did some PR work, then joined a firm that arranged exhibitions, then became a dental receptionist. 'The dentist was a friend of mine, Jonathan Portner. When he set up on his own, he asked if I'd like to help him part time, which I did for many years.'

Footballers, then and now, don't normally care for their wives going out to work, preferring them to be there in the afternoons when they return home with bruised shins and bruised egos.

'Oh I was all for Bonnie going back to work again,' says Joe. 'Jonathan was my dentist as well, and a friend. They're still great friends. I have only one thing against him – he supports Arsenal. Absolutely potty about the Gunners.

'The times I've had to sit and suffer in his dentist's chair and hear him grinding on about the Double team, about Charlie George this, John Radford that. The pain of him droning on was far worse than the pain of his drill. In a dentist's chair, you can't stop them rabbiting on. So it was bloody agony, listening to all the Arsenal stuff. I often wanted to ram his drill down his throat.

'Apart from that, I was well pleased. He's a good bloke, and a good dentist. I was happy that Bonnie was working with him and enjoying it.'

'Naturally I became a Spurs fan, on meeting Joe,' says Bonnie. 'Once I'd got used to the idea that Spurs would always come first, I came to enjoy all the big occasions. It was very exciting, going to all those cup finals.

'I didn't actually watch him in any of his games for Ireland. I just never seemed to be able to go and see him. I used to joke that he could easily have a wife and six kids in Ireland, for all I knew.

'Joe playing for Spurs, gave us a great social life, being invited everywhere. I had a great time. I met Diana Ross through Joe, which I would never have done otherwise. Oh and lots of other show-business people.

'I saw a lot of him of course, as he was home by two o'clock most days. Not like the life of a football manager. I'd rather be a player's wife than a manager's wife, I can tell you.

'But at the time, I had no idea what he might do after his playing career was over. It was something I gradually began to think about, worrying what he might do for the rest of his life.'

Chapter Twelve

I did have competition for my place in the Spurs team, mainly from Ray Evans, but for three years, after Ray's first-team debut in 1969 when I'd been injured, I kept Ray out. I came back as the first-choice right back.

But I was injured again in 1972. Ray came in, played well, and had a good run. When I got better, I thought I would naturally get my place back, as by then I was a senior player. But it didn't happen. I was in and out from then on.

My worst disappointment ever at Spurs was the UEFA Cup final of 1974 – against Feyenoord. It would have been my fifth cup final. I wasn't picked for the first leg at White Hart Lane which we drew 2-2. Ray was in. I hadn't been in the team for most of the season, with injuries, but I still hoped to make it.

I was trying to get back after a long spell of injury and was struggling to get fit, but I wasn't even named as sub for the final in Holland. That was the time there was a riot. Spurs fans had been fighting on the boat across and were still causing trouble when the match started. Bill came on the pitch and appealed to our supporters for calm.

We got beaten 2-0. I went up for my medal, my runners' up medal, as I'd played in enough of the earlier rounds to qualify. I've no idea where it went. Truly. I either left it on the pitch or in the dressing room. Whatever happened, I never brought it home. I was so disgusted. It was the first final I hadn't played in for Spurs, in all my seasons as a professional at the club. And it was the first time during that period that Spurs had lost in a final. Five finals – and the only one I didn't play in we got beat. No, that didn't cheer me up. I was just too upset.

I suppose what was really happening was that it was the end of an era. Everything at the club was changing. The team I'd joined, and been established in for a good five years, had begun to break up. People were drifting away. Spurs were not doing as well as they had done. I'd seen five years at the top, grown used to being an established player, and being in a successful team, who won pots. Now I was beginning to see the other side. A team not doing so well – and I wasn't sure of being in it. And I was getting near the age of 30.

I asked for a transfer. Bill and Eddie said no, they wouldn't let me go. I had to honour my contract. If I worked hard, I would regain my form.

I didn't think I had lost form, but then you don't. You can't see that you're doing anything different. You seem to be doing the same as always, working hard, doing the same things. I couldn't understand what they were on about. I can now. But not at the time. At the time, it seemed to me the whole team wasn't performing well, not just me. Yet they were dropping me all the time. For years, the team had picked itself. Each week, barring injuries, it had been roughly the same line-up: Jennings, Kinnear, Knowles, Mullery, England, Beal, Gilzean, Perryman, Chivers, Peters. Well, Mullers had left in 1972, with Martin Peters taking over as captain. Those were the players I had played with for so long. But by 1974, I was beginning to feel not part of them any more.

When you have a so-called loss of form, it affects your whole way of thinking. You have been immersed in your own self importance, as an established first-team player, then suddenly you are out. So you begin to have self-doubts.

In my years as manager, I've tried to look back to those experiences, to remember how I felt when I was out of the team, what I was told, how I handled it. It is very difficult, handling a player who has lost form. When you're struggling to get results on a weekly basis, you can't afford to keep someone in the team who's not performing. If the team's winning, that's a bit easier. You can carry someone in a winning team. Dean Holdsworth once had a big drop in form. One season he was on fire, banging in the goals, then it all dried up.

The first thing I do when this happens is draw them out of the limelight. The press and the supporters have usually been getting on at them, so I give them a breather. I tell them this, why I'm doing it. I tell them I still have faith in them, put an arm round them, but I'm taking them out of the limelight till their confidence is back. I can say they've got an injury, so everyone doesn't know they've been dropped. Or now that there are bigger squads, a manager can say he's working on a rotation system – that's a good excuse. Then I tell them they must work extra hard in training, to get it all back.

The second thing you can do, if a vital player has lost form, is rearrange the team or the tactics. You might move them to a position or a role with less pressure. When Marcus Gayle lost form, I moved him out of the middle of the attack and onto the wing, where he wasn't under the same pressure.

When it happened to me, all those years ago, nothing was explained, no reasons given, no attempt made to help me. I was just dropped. No ifs and buts. That was it, end of story. It was clear to everyone you'd been dropped – to the rest of the team, to the fans. In my day, there was no cover from the manager. Your failure was public.

Bill himself was coming to the end of his time. His touch was probably failing. He didn't seem in tune with all the new things happening, the new tactics, the new attitudes, the new ways of doing things, off and on the pitch. He'd begun to say it himself, lots of times, that he didn't like the way football was going, all the money coming in, all the greed and commercialization. In his day, so he was always telling us, people played for the love of the game, as he had done.

The 1973-4 season was pretty horrendous. We ended 11th in the First Division. The next season began very badly. It was clear Bill would be going soon.

He did once discuss with me who I thought should take over. His idea was to hand it on to Johnny Giles and Danny Blanchflower –

Johnny as player-manager, Danny as sort of general manager. I thought this was a good idea. I admired both of them, and had played with both of them. Johnny had been player-manager of Ireland for a time.

I discussed with Bill the chances of me joining the staff in some capacity. He said it was a hard job, coaching, trying to keep everyone happy. But he was quite encouraging. Me and Bill used to discuss players a lot, the younger ones coming through, how they were developing, what their chances were. One of them was Glenn Hoddle who became a Spurs apprentice in 1974. Yes, you didn't have to be a genius to recognize his natural talents.

In my mind, I saw myself as being a youth coach, then slowly coming up through the ranks and one day managing Spurs. That was my fantasy.

Then Bill resigned in September 1974. I don't think he was pushed, but he might have been given a nudge. He'd bought a few players who hadn't quite worked out, such as David Jenkins from Arsenal. That didn't help. But his end was coming, we all knew that. It couldn't go on.

He wasn't of course going anywhere else. How could he? He loved Spurs too much, had given his life to Spurs. He created that Double team of 1960-61 that no one will ever forget, and went on to win another five major cups. So he just retired. I think they made him Hon. President or something, but it wasn't really handled very well, not very dignified. I felt sorry for Bill, the way he just seemed to be allowed to creep out of the club.

Johnny Giles and Danny didn't of course get the manager's job. I've spoken to Giles about it recently – and he says that it was a serious offer, at least he thought it was at the time. Bill Nick had spoken to him about it several times. But when Bill suggested it to the club, they said piss off, it's nothing to do with you, who do you think you are, we'll pick the next manager.

In those days, a manager who'd had great success, like say Bill Shankley at Liverpool, did manage to organize the next manager, or help pick his successor. Bill Nick was only doing what he thought was best for the club, a club he'd worked for all his life, for almost

40 years, since he'd joined as a boy of 16 in 1936. He'd been totally loyal to them. And what did they say? What amounted to get lost. Instead in came Terry Neil – from Arsenal.

By the end of that season, 1974-75, we had dropped to 19th, one place above the relegation zone. I wasn't playing in the first half of the season, not till after Christmas, then I kept my place till the end of the season.

It all hinged on the last match. We needed to win to stay up – at home against Leeds, in front of 50,000, on 29 April 1975. We managed it, 4-2. Cyril Knowles got two goals, one from a penalty. The other two came from Martin Chivers and Alfie Conn. Johnny Giles was in the Leeds team that day. I knew him well because we roomed together for Ireland.

It mattered so much to us, not to get beaten. No player wants to have 'relegated' on their CV. And of course Terry Neil didn't want to be known as the manager who took us down. But I have to say, Leeds didn't play all that hard that day. No, they didn't let us win. But they were, let's say, a bit soft. Johnny said to me afterwards, 'Thank your lucky stars we had nothing to play for.' So we finished the season all feeling very relieved.

I came in for pre-season training, in the summer of 1975, and was told by Terry Neil that Brighton had put in a bid of £40,000 for me.

Terry Neil had bought in Don McAllister and he was now playing in the back four. He'd cost £80,000 from Bolton. I remember him bringing his own hairdryer into the dressing room. He brought it in his bag and took it out to do his hair, which was very blond, so we naturally called him a woofter. He wasn't – that was just a way of getting at him, winding him up as a new player.

I didn't think he was better than me, but he was younger. It was clear I was going to be stuck in the reserves. That was no use to me, no future in that. So, there didn't seem much point in staying at Spurs.

I rang Phil Beal. He'd already gone to Brighton, and asked him what they were like. He said they were a good team, with good support, very ambitious, with a good chance of doing well, getting back in the First Division. They had some experienced players like

Sammy Morgan, Brian Horton, Chris Cattlin, and Peter Grummitt. So I agreed to go to Brighton.

I was aged 28. I'd been at Spurs 12 seasons, since signing as an amateur. Despite losing over one year with my broken leg, I'd had five or six years as a regular, been a winner in four cup finals. So I'd done well, when you think of that disappointment at not being taken on by Watford at 16. I'd had a good career, at a top club, one of the glamour teams of the times.

I'll always be grateful to Bill Nicholson. He took me on, gave me a second chance after the Watford rejection. During my time in his first team, he always stood by me. He could easily have replaced me by buying someone new, but he never did. I was lucky, playing under Bill.

But in the end, the luck ran out. The timing was all wrong. When I came to the end, Bill had left. If he'd stayed another year, I might have got a coaching job, then worked my way up. When Terry Neil came, I had no connection with him. I wasn't in his plans, either for his team or on the coaching side. So that was it. I was out. Time to move on.

Chapter Thirteen

It was during the second half of 1999 that Joe was telling me all that, telling me the story of his life and career up to the end of his Tottenham days. I had lots of sessions with him, going to his North London house, as he had lots of spare time, slowly recovering his health after his heart attack, getting back to full fitness. While he remembered times past there was also a running story going on. His energy was returning, both physical and mental, thoughts stirring, plans beginning to form in his mind.

Some days he seemed pretty fed up, bored rigid with hanging around all day, with nothing to do except be sensible and conserve energy, which he found very hard to do.

I arrived early one day and found him outside, looking very cheesed off, putting out the dustbin. Bonnie, his wife, had gone to Hampstead for the morning to attend a history of art lecture. It was on 19thy-century architecture, which she wasn't looking forward to, but she was probably quite pleased, as it got her out of the house and the sight of Joe moping around.

But the next time I called, he was all beams and smiles. He had been out to watch a game or two and had changed his answerphone message so that his recorded voice could now be heard cheerfully announcing, 'I am fit, I am able, I am raring to go.'

Over the years, Joe has made a speciality of leaving personal messages for anyone ringing him. I remember a couple of years ago when he was at Wimbledon, winning Manager of the Month awards, ringing him and hearing his voice saying, 'I can't answer you at the moment, but if it's the chairman of Juventus, Barcelona or Real Madrid, don't worry, I'll ring you right back ...'

It seemed daft to me, when he hadn't quite fully recovered, to be encouraging the football world to contact him again. His home phone number, like that of any Premier League manager, even one temporarily resting, is of course only known to the chosen, which means other managers, his own star players, the top agents and a selected few from the football media. Yet here he was, clearly waiting for the call to come – the call which would bring him back to full-time craziness, countless worries, anxieties, frustrations, fear and assorted loathings, all of which had clearly contributed to the drama that had recently happened in his life, plus of course the joy, the camaraderie, excitement, exhilaration and assorted laughs which football can provide.

From then on, every time I went so see him, the phone would go constantly while we talked. It was all a bit eerie, as his own jovial recorded message could be heard booming out first, like that awful demented laughing policeman record my mother used to love and I hated. Then would come the more hesitant, disembodied voice of the person leaving a message. Both were on at top volume, so Joe could hear whoever it was from wherever he was in the house. He didn't appear to be aware of the noise, only pricking up his ears if it sounded particularly interesting.

'I've had one possible job suggested so far,' he said one day. 'Manager of Besitkas in Turkey. David Dein of Arsenal told me about this. He lives not far from me, and I know him very well, but I happened to meet him at Wembley, for the England game against Luxembourg. He was there with the chairman of Besitkas. Afterwards, David said they might be interested in me. So I says I'll think about it. 'I talked to Graeme Souness who used to be in Turkey, managing Galatasaray, and he said it's a madness, they'll eat you alive, two defeats and they hate you. But they pay well. I said oh yeah, but then do you actually get your money at the end? "Most of it," said Graeme. "They'll argue, but then compromise on a sum, but it'll still be worth it."

'I know about the two main Turkish clubs, but I don't know much about their players. But anyway, I was thinking about it, weighing it up, finding out as much as I could. I then hear they'll pay £750,000 plus bonuses, which could be one million a year. Bloody hell, I thought that is worth considering. David Dein had gone out of his way to help. I'll never forget that.

'I came home and told Bonnie and she said no way, she's not going to Turkey, no chance. Well I'm not going on my own, am I, so I told them thanks, but no thanks.'

The reference to Souness was interesting because he was another top manager, with Premiership experience, then out of work, who had also played for Spurs. He had recently come through the trauma of heart surgery. Other well-known managers, also unemployed at that time, included Glenn Hoddle and Terry Venables, yet again famous former players with Spurs' connections. They looked as if they would be joined by Brian Kidd as Blackburn had had a run of poor results. All the papers were tipping Joe to be about first in line for the job, should it come up.

Had he heard anything, directly or indirectly? 'My agent did get a call a few days ago from someone at Blackburn, asking if I was free, or if I was still tied in some way to Wimbledon. He says no, I'm free and fit and ready to go. So he asks if I would be interested. My agent says I might be, but I have got other offers. They then asked if I'd come for an interview. I said I might, but they should know about my CV by now.

'This was all hush-hush. Not to be repeated, as Brian is still there. But they did add that I'd turned them down once before, before Brian Kidd was appointed, which they hadn't forgotten. This was a year or so ago and they didn't actually approach me direct. I'm told someone at Wimbledon turned it down on my behalf. Anyway, it's a good sign, don't you think? That they're still thinking of me.'

There had also been an approach, so Joe said, on behalf of

another top club. No wonder he had been beaming, thinking he might be about to be offered something tempting. This call had been overtly just a routine, informal chat, asking an intermediary about Joe's management style and talents. All very elliptical, but this is what happens in football. In each case, the manager still had his job, and presumably knew little about any backstairs goings-on.

I asked if say Villa and Blackburn came up, both in the news that week, and he could take his pick, which would he choose?

'They're both good, big clubs. One attraction of Blackburn is that Jack Walker has lots of mone to invest in buying players. And I also know from talking to people he doesn't interfere. He's not there from day to day as he lives in Jersey

'On the other hand, Blackburn's in the First Division. It will be a struggle getting them up. They're in a position they never should have been. And Blackburn is a long way away. I'd have to go and live there, find myself a house or flat. Bonnie wouldn't move from here, not now, not after what she's been through. I'd come home to London after Saturday's match, wherever it was. I'd stay at home till Sunday or Monday morning – then have the whole week up there. It could work okay – I'm used to travelling.

'The big attraction of Villa is that they are in the Premier League. Deadly Doug seems to be a hands-on chairman, there all the time. But he couldn't be more involved than Sam. No chairman is. He lived for Wimbledon, was in the dressing room all the time, watching training, everything. But he never interfered in tactics or with players. I will say that.'

What about the money? Which did he think would pay better? If of course that was a consideration.

'That doesn't matter. You would be well paid by both clubs. I guess about £600,000 per year would be the going rate. But both chairmen would give you the chance of glory. And that's what it's all about – you can't buy that.'

But which would be the bigger challenge, which would you feel most satisfied with, if you did it well?

'Well, Villa should be a top-six club. The potential is there. But with Blackburn, you think was it a one-off, winning the Premiership? Are they really a Premier League club? And what sort of talent have they got there anyway?

'Yeah, it's quite interesting, weighing them up. Gives me something to think about. Who knows what will happen ... I don't believe everything I read in the papers.'

Joe was also receiving calls from players, either to wish him a speedy recovery, to find out the latest gen about the rumours, or just to establish contact again. Dennis Wise, captain of Chelsea and an old friend of Joe's from his Wimbledon days, was often on the phone, ringing mainly just for chats.

'I've also just had a call from Robbie Earl [captain of Wimbledon]. He said not to forget him, wherever I might go. He reminded me he wants to go into coaching. I asked him if he was sure. I said there's not the same money in coaching as playing. You won't get £20,000 a week coaching, the way you can as a player. You have to start at the bottom. It's tough, very hard to progress. Robbie said yeah, but he was willing to start at the bottom. He just wanted to carry on in football and learn his trade. I think one day he will make a good manager.

'Then I had John Hartson on the phone. I've been rubbished for having paid £7 million for him, so it's nice he's now come good, scoring the goals I knew he would, with people now wanting him.

'George Graham is after him. So John was wanting my advice. "What do you think I should do, Gaffer?" I said that Spurs is a better team, bigger club, better set-up. You won't be fighting relegation every season, you'll be expected to win trophies.

'I asked him what it had been like when he played under George at Arsenal, if they'd got on well. "It was George who put me in the team." There you go, I said. If it comes up, go for it.

'I gather that Spurs are talking about £6 million for Hartson, plus John Scales and Jose Dominguez thrown in. Sam has said no chance. I agree with him. Scales has been at Wimbledon before and there's no need to have him back. Dominguez is not a

Wimbledon player, is he? I think Sam is holding out for £10 million, in cash, no exchange of players.

'If Chris Sutton can cost £10 million, then why not Hartson? If I had to bet who in the end will score more goals in the Premiership, I know who my money would be on. We'll see what happens about John Hartson. And we'll see what happens elsewhere ...'

Joe was not feeling so well when I arrived next time, complaining about feeling rotten. He thought it might be flu, plus indigestion. Bonnie said he should go and have some tests, just to make sure, if he was getting worried. But of course it was his own fault, having gone off to Dublin the week before, no doubt staying up late with his old Irish friends.

This was one of the more entertaining, if minor, new developments – a regular shot of RTE, the Irish national television company, acting as a studio expert and commentator, mainly covering the European games involving British clubs.

Now that he was recovering, Joe had received many offers of television work, being a fluent and amusing talker, a good reader of the game, with an inside knowledge, still up to date, but he had refused most requests, apart from making an FA Cup draw and doing a few interviews. He felt he would soon be back as a manager in the English league, so it might not be too clever to go on the BBC, ITV or Sky, criticizing or even rubbishing some player, some club, some chairman, whom he might be about to deal with and work with professionally. But giving his opinions on an Irish channel, that was something he loved doing. It was also a welcome distraction, going off to Dublin one night a week, doing the programme, staying the night in a hotel, meeting up with his old chums, Johnny Giles and Eamonn Dunphy.

Joe did his homework in advance, watched lots of videos, learned about various European clubs and players he didn't know much about, all of which should come in handy in the future. But Bonnie was not so pleased. She knew that meeting his old chums would be bound to lead to the odd drink or two, just when he'd got his weight under control.

The recent match he'd covered for RTE had been Ireland v. Turkey, by chance the fixture he had first appeared in himself, all those years ago. This time it was the deciding game to see which one would qualify for Euro 2000. Alas, Ireland didn't.

'At the match, I met Bobby Robson. I asked him what he was doing here. He said he was looking at Hakan Sukur, Turkey's centre forward. I said he is pretty good. I'd had a look some time ago at another Turkish player, their centre half, but I'd worried about one thing – you never hear of any Turk who has done well abroad. They are brilliant at home, very impressive, but they don't travel. It will happen some time, but not yet. Bobby agreed with me, but he said he could only afford such players, they were not too expensive. And even so, he'd need to sell some of the players left behind by Gullitt. They'd cost millions to buy, but were worth far less, sitting in the reserves. You got the impression that some were not even trying any more. He'd have to let them go on a free transfer in the end – perhaps even pay some of them to leave. I said, get their agents to work on it, surely you can get some of the money back. No need to give them away. He did seem pretty depressed about the situation he'd been left with.

'I know the problem about shopping around for bargains. You can get foreign players cheap, but you are taking a chance, unless they are top class like the ones at Chelsea and Arsenal for example. Not many of them are good travellers. I only bought one foreigner at Wimbledon, that was the Norwegian, Leonhardsen. Scandinavians are not such a problem. They can all speak English and adapt well to the country and the English game.

'I said to Bobby he should look in the English First Division. There really isn't such a difference in class amongst some of the clubs there and in the Premier League. He could get a striker there who would be thrilled to go to Newcastle, would play his bollocks off, try really hard. With an unknown foreigner, you never knew. It's all a matter of luck.

'I also asked Bobby about Warren Barton, whom I sold to

Kevin Keegan. He came through the same sort of route as I did, having trials with a professional club and at first being rejected. Bobby said he was very pleased with him – Warren was a model professional. Bobby asked me about Carl Cort, Jason Euelle and Michael Hughes.'

As the year had moved on, Joe had also been keeping in touch by going more regularly to English games. 'I went to see Arsenal against Newcastle. It was a 0-0 draw. Not the best game I've ever seen. It wasn't just that Newcastle had come to defend, but that Arsenal had run out of ideas on how to break them down.

'I talked to Wenger afterwards and he was shaking his head. He couldn't believe Arsenal had played so badly, couldn't work out why they'd been so disappointing. I said to him, "I've had Saturdays like that." And he just smiled.'

PART TWO

Brighton and the World

Chapter Fourteen

I signed for Brighton and Hove Albion in August 1975. The transfer fee was officially £40,000. That's what was announced, a reasonably average sum for the times, but it was agreed that I would get it all. Normally, with a transfer fee at the time, a player only got a small percentage. I think it was really a sort of thank you, for the years of loyal service. I didn't get it in one lump. It was to be spread of several years, as part of my salary. I paid tax on it all, in the normal way.

The manager was Peter Taylor, well known as Brian Clough's partner at Notts Forest, a goalkeeper in his time. He had worked his way up with Cloughy through various management jobs. While Clough was front of house, the public face, Peter was in the background, doing much of the donkey work. Cloughy had left Brighton and Peter was now manager on his own.

We kept on our home in London, in Woodside Park, Mill Hill, at least for the time being. I decided I could commute by train each day to Brighton, getting off at Hove, returning in the afternoon after training. On match days, Bonnie would come to watch me. We'd have a meal in Brighton after the match, then come back to London together. That was the plan.

When I arrived at Brighton for the first training sessions, I did still worry if I'd done the right thing. My pride had been hurt by being transferred. I still wondered if I should have stayed, played in the reserves, fought to get my place back. But I couldn't have faced the reserves any more.

I actually thought I should not just have been kept – I should have been made captain. Pat Jennings and I were the two senior pros, the last of the old Cup-winning team. Everyone else was new. I'd won honours, they hadn't. Then I thought well, that era is over, you can't turn the clock back. There's a new gang in charge. Best to move on; best to have a new challenge.

But I knew it was a come-down, going to a smaller club, in a lower league, down in the Third Division, after the glamour of Spurs. Still, Phil had told me the club was ambitious and had a good set up. It turned out to be not quite what I expected.

First of all, Peter Taylor was hardly there. Dunno where he was, what he was doing, but we only saw him on Fridays after training, then on Saturday at the match.

Second, we didn't have our own training ground. We'd assemble at the Goldstone Ground, the club's stadium in Hove, which wasn't bad, but we very rarely trained there. Instead we'd jog for 15 minutes or so through the streets and do our training on a public park. There would be dogs walking over the pitch, mums with prams. There weren't even any goalposts. We just had cones on the ground or a pile of bibs.

Third, the coaching was mostly a joke, when you consider it was a so-called professional club with paid coaches. I don't know how one of the coaches got his job. We called him the Spud Man. We were told that he sold potatoes, that was his real job. Apparently he'd been providing Cloughy and Peter Taylor with potatoes. He had a job as a coach. That's what we heard anyway. I'm sure it was just a joke. But it was clear all the same that he had little idea about coaching.

There were about 16 professionals and when the Spud Man was angry with us, because we hadn't done something right, as a punishment he would make us run the 400 yards or so across the park to this phone box. Just an ordinary red telephone box. 'Get your arses up there at once,' he'd shout at us.

We'd have to go there and back, six times, but on the first circuit, one of us would hide behind the telephone box. He'd stay there, have a good rest, till the next circuit. Next time, someone else would have a rest. When it was obvious the Spud Man hadn't noticed, then two of us would stay behind the phone box. Then eventually it became four – till in the end only half of us was doing the running, but he didn't seem to twig it.

In the first season I was there, we did quite well. We were on the fringes of promotion to the Second Division. Then in an away match at Port Vale, I got tackled by their left winger. Not a nasty tackle, but I did my cruciate ligaments. My knee got twisted round, ending back to front. I'd snapped the ligaments. That was it, stretchered off.

I couldn't play for six months. I could have had an operation, but I was told the success rate was only 50-50. Today, it's a bit simpler. They can take ligaments out of your calf and there's a much bigger success rate. I did try to come back and started training again. I had my leg all strapped up, but I was still limping. Then I had a brace, but it was agony every time and it just swelled up.

I'd begun by then to get on quite well with Peter. He'd call me in to discuss the team, who should be played, what tactics. We chatted generally about ideas, how football should be played, or discussed the opposition, their strengths and weaknesses. I did tell Peter that I fancied going into coaching. He was quite encouraging.

Then he left. I'm not sure if he got the sack, or just packed it in. But anyway that was it, he was gone.

If I'd been stronger at the time, as a person, and more confident, I might have asked what the chances were of me being considered for manager. But I didn't say anything, I didn't push myself forward. The chairman, Mike Bamber, did call me in and told me who they were thinking of appointing – Alan Mullery. He asked me what he was like, as I'd played with him at Spurs. I said his pedigree is terrific – Spurs captain, England captain – can't get a better CV than that.

So he was appointed. I was looking forward to working with him again – I hoped that as I knew him, and had been his team-mate, he'd give me some sort of coaching job. That was my hope. But then when he arrived he'd brought his own coaching staff. So that was that.

Once again, the timing was all wrong. I was the wrong person, in the wrong place, at the wrong time. My fantasy of getting started on a coaching career seemed doomed. Not only that: because of my injury, it was inevitable I'd have to leave.

THE LINE UP

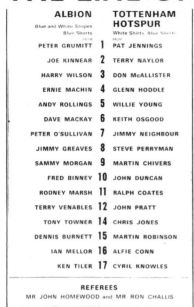

ALBION Blue and White Stripes Blue Shorts		TOTTENHAM HOTSPUR White Shirts, Blue Shorts
PETER GRUMITT	1	PAT JENNINGS
JOE KINNEAR	2	TERRY NAYLOR
HARRY WILSON	3	DON McALLISTER
ERNIE MACHIN	4	GLENN HODDLE
ANDY ROLLINGS	5	WILLIE YOUNG
DAVE MACKAY	6	KEITH OSGOOD
PETER O'SULLIVAN	7	JIMMY NEIGHBOUR
JIMMY GREAVES	8	STEVE PERRYMAN
SAMMY MORGAN	9	MARTIN CHIVERS
FRED BINNEY	10	JOHN DUNCAN
RODNEY MARSH	11	RALPH COATES
TERRY VENABLES	12	JOHN PRATT
TONY TOWNER	14	CHRIS JONES
DENNIS BURNETT	15	MARTIN ROBINSON
IAN MELLOR	16	ALFIE CONN
KEN TILER	17	CYRIL KNOWLES

REFEREES
MR. JOHN HOMEWOOD and MR. RON CHALLIS

JOE KINNEAR

TESTIMONIAL MATCH

BRIGHTON & HOVE

ALBION

v

TOTTENHAM HOTSPUR

On Brighton & Hove Albion Ground

TUESDAY, 23rd MARCH, 1976

Kick-off 7.30 p.m.

Official Souvenir Programme **10p**

From the programme of Joe's testimonial match against Spurs:
March 1976.

My knee was never going to get any better, so my playing career was over. And my coaching career had never even got started. I was heartbroken. I'd only played 16 times for Brighton, in those couple of seasons, though I did score one goal – unusual for me. Now I was out of football, and also out of a job.

Alan did help me sort out some compensation, so that was something. I got nothing from the PFA. I'd paid my subs for years but got sod all. I got £10,000 from Brighton, as compensation, to pay off my contract. And I'd got a testimonial match against Spurs which made me about £6,000.

So I was reasonably well off. I also still had my two houses, the ones in Watford I'd bought and was renting out. I wasn't going to starve in the near future. For the times, I had done quite well. Not like today. A person with the career I had in the top division, and retiring at the age I did, would have millions in the bank today, with no need to work ever again. Many players from my era retired with

Left: Joe aged 2, at his grandmother's house in Dublin.

Below: Before playing on South Oxhey playing fields for the Watford Boys team in the 1960/1 season (front row, third from the right).

Bottom: Lining up for the Watford Sunday County team in 1962 (front row, second from the right).

Joe in 1966, as a young professional at Spurs.
©*Sunday Express*

Bill Nicholson at the gates to White Hart Lane.
©Peter Robinson/ Empics

Off to a good start, winning with the Tottenham youth team in Holland, 1965 (front row, third from the right).

Taking his place in the team photo shoot after Spurs won the FA Cup in 1967, beating Chelsea 2-1 (back row from left): Joe Kinnear, Cyril Knowles, Mike England, Pat Jennings, Alan Gilzean, Alan Mullery. Front row from left: Jimmy Robertson, Jimmy Greaves, Dave Mackay, Terry Venables, Frank Saul.

Celebrating victory over Wolves in the all-English UEFA Cup final in 1972.

Joe with his mother Greta, in 1970.

Surrounded by his four sisters in the Cup final year, 1967. From left to right: Shirley, Amelia, Louise and Carmen. ©Owen Barnes

Buying cars in Watford with Bonnie in 1972. ©*Watford Observer*

Joe with Bonnie in her boutique, Fella, in fashionable Hampstead in the early seventies. ©*Daily Mirror*

Playing for the Republic of Ireland in 1974.

Joe with (from left to right) Bobby Moore, Cyril Knowles, Diana Ross and Pat Jennings.

Cracking open the champagne at his testimonial for Brighton, against Spurs in 1977, with (left to right) Rodney Marsh, Terry Venables, Dave Mackay and Jimmy Greaves.

In Dubai, at a charity match in 1986.

Dave Mackay and Joe take in the delights of the Belle Vue ground, home of Doncaster Rovers, in 1987. ©Phil Callaghan

With the Doncaster team in the same year, Joe as assistant manager.

nothing at all, having wasted what little they'd earned enjoying themselves or just spent most of it on day-to-day living.

So I had to find some sort of job. I had no income, apart from the rents and I couldn't live off them. But I didn't know what to do. All I was staring at was the dole queue ...

Chapter Fifteen

When I finished at Brighton in 1977, there didn't seem to be many things I could do. I'd left school with no qualifications and I'd never finished my apprenticeship in the print.

So I decided to do what countless footballers have done over the years – I bought a pub. After all, what else have you got, apart from your name, which for a while quite a lot of blokes in certain places will remember. Alex Ferguson did the same, when his playing career was over and it didn't look as if he would get into management.

I took over the tenancy of The Stag in the middle of Watford. I think it cost me six grand, but I spent a lot converting it. My idea was to make it into a football pub, or at least a sports bar. So I knocked the walls about and covered them in football photos and sporting prints.

But before I realized it, it had become an Irish pub, which I hadn't even planned. It just happened that all the local Irish started going there. I suppose because I'd played 26 times for Ireland, that must have been why. When I saw the way things were going, I converted it into an Irish pub. Every weekend, I'd have a live Irish band, who did either traditional Irish music or country and western. I also changed the juke-box, which just used to have rock and roll. I made it all Irish music. The result was that we were packed out. Big success.

Bonnie wasn't involved, although she had more business experience than me. She didn't care for it. And when she did turn up, the Irish punters would say to me, 'Is your missus foreign then?' Bonnie does have a proper educated English accent, unlike me. They couldn't understand her, and she couldn't understand them. But they could understand me. Funny, that.

I put a couple in charge, as managers, and they lived in a flat above the pub. So they were always there. I turned up three times a week and signed autographs, and had my photo taken by the punters.

I usually went there at weekends as well, when it was busiest, to keep an eye on things. And I saw quite a few punch-ups. When there was a big Gaelic football match on, they would all come to the pub wearing their colours, supporting Tipperary or whoever it was against a Dublin club. They'd all listen in the pub on a short-wave radio, cheering on their teams. If the Dublin team won, they'd all hate the Jackeens. That's what country people call people from Dublin. Someone would pour a pint of Guinness over a Jackeen's head, a few punches would be exchanged, then tables and chairs would be flying all over the place.

But one thing about Irish people, they soon forgive and forget. They'd go home with bloody noses, but next morning, at opening time, they'd be back, with their black eyes and sore heads, drinking and talking with the people they'd been fighting the night before, as if nothing had happened.

They were rivals, but didn't really hate each other. Not like say Spurs and Arsenal fans. You don't get Spurs fans and Arsenal fans drinking in the same pub.

I did think of opening a string of Irish pubs, because mine was going so well. It would have been a novelty then, 20 years ago. Now they are everywhere. But it was just an idea, I didn't do anything about it.

At the back of my mind, I was still thinking about doing something in football, using some of my experience. Anything really, I wasn't fussy. Now and again I rang up about odd coaching jobs, when I thought there might be a vacancy, looking after youth teams. But I had no luck.

In those days, coaching the youth team was a secure job. You had it for years, unless you did something really wrong. You were nurturing young players, for the long term, so you were left to it. The *success or failure of the first team didn't affect you. It meant in those days that few jobs came up. Now, there's no security at any level in coaching. A new manager very often brings in a whole team, all the way down, so you are out, whoever you are.*

Now and again I contacted people I'd known, if I saw them getting management jobs, in the hope they might have something for me. I rang Terry Venables when he took over at QPR, about the possibility of a job coaching the youth team. I just missed out. Terry had given the job to his old friend, George Graham. George then went from that job to manage Millwall – and the rest is football history ...

In the end, just to keep my hand in, I took a part-time job as player-coach of Woodford Town in the Southern League. I shouldn't really have even thought of trying to play again. My leg was agony. I did play a few times, strapped up, but even playing with a limp to ease some of the pain didn't work. So I just stuck to the coaching side.

There was a manager there, Bill Caldwell, but he left the coaching to me. It only meant two nights a week, Tuesday and Thursday, after the players had finished their day jobs as bricklayers, plumbers or whatever.

The owner of the club was a bloke called Bill Larkin. He was the peanut king. You ain't heard of Larkin's Roasted Peanuts? Oh they were famous. As famous as Percy Dalton's. He'd bought the club and converted the little stand so it had a nightclub underneath, which they called Woodies. The idea was that the proceeds from the nightclub would fund the football club. The nightclub was popular with a lot of ex-West Ham players who used to come along, like Bobby Moore and Frank Lampard. It had a licence till two in the morning. It was always packed.

But the trouble with the nightclub being part of the football club was that the players would go into it after training. Don't forget we only trained in the evenings. So they'd do two hours' hard training, working well enough, then go into the club and get pissed out of their heads. Well some of them did.

One of the players I got for the club was Jimmy Greaves. I think we paid him about £250 a week, which was about 10 times what the rest were getting, but he put a few hundred more on our gates. Jimmy was having a hard time. He'd been out of football really, but I persuaded him to come back. He'd given up the drinking, but I think he was still having treatment. So our club, with its own night-club, was perhaps not the best place for him. He did get depressed a lot. I also signed his son Danny, so we had two Greavesies, playing together. The team wasn't bad. I had Ernie Tippett, whom I later took to Wimbledon, as youth team coach.

Coaching the team fitted in well with running the pub, but it wasn't much of a springboard for getting back into the Football League. The only way to do that, so I was told, was to get some proper coaching qualifications. As a player, I had dismissed the idea. I thought I knew it all. I'd played at the top, won Cup Final medals, played for Ireland, what good would it do me? But slowly it was becoming clear that I wasn't going to get anywhere without an FA badge.

I started an FA course in 1980, but didn't finish it first time. I can't remember what happened, what else I was doing. Anyway, I did it all in 1983. I passed and got the coaching certificate.

Then one day not long afterwards I got a call from the FA. They said would I be interested in coaching abroad. I said I hadn't thought of it. I'd rather have coached in Britain, but I said I'd be interested in anything, anywhere, if it was a proper coaching job, just to get back into football. They said they'd let me know, if anything came up.

I was standing in the kitchen one day, with Bonnie, and a voice on the telephone asks me if I'd like to coach in Nepal. I thought it was someone messing around. Katmandu, they said, that was where the job was. I was then sure it was a wind up. I'd heard of Katmandu, but thought it was a joke place that didn't exist. This voice said no, it's straight up, they're looking for a qualified coach.

I said I'd talk to Bonnie about it and let them know. So we discussed it. She said I should at least go out there, see what the job entailed, without committing myself.

Nepal was apparently preparing for the Asian Games and they wanted a national coach. I was told this royal prince was in charge of their FA, so it was a sort of government job, or at least a royal job. That meant there would be a chance that I'd actually get paid.

The money wasn't much. From memory, I think they were offering me three months' work for £12,000. About £1,000 a week. Not huge, but not bad. I'm not going to get far in football being a coach, not even a manager, with a little non-league team. And I can easily leave the pub for three months and it shouldn't come to harm.

I'd got it into my head I wanted some more experience as a coach. This was all that had turned up. So I thought why not, go out there, see what it's all about ...

Chapter Sixteen

I went out to Nepal to check it out – and it was just unbelievable. Mind boggling. I had never been to such a place, or met such people. They were so beautiful, such spiritual people. There were all these castes, some people wore red dots on their foreheads, dunno what they each were, Hindus, Muslims or Buddhists, or whatever. Absolutely fascinating.

It's just a little country, about 14 million, very wild and mountainous, all on the slopes of the Himalayas. The roads were terrible, the transport hellish. It was like going back centuries. In the main street of Katmandu, the capital, there were sheep and goats, just walking around, roaming free. The cars had to dodge round them. Once you left the middle of the town, that was it, you were out in the wilds. There was no electricity, no telephones, no televisions, not out in the country. People carted their water home by hand from the well.

It was quite a culture shock for me. I had honestly thought that the rest of the world lived like England. Not that I'd really thought about it. As a Spurs player, or playing for Ireland, I had travelled to lots of places, all over Europe and elsewhere, but you know what it's like – you travel, but you don't go anywhere. You just sit on the coach playing cards, as you would at home. You stay in a hotel bedroom, very much like all the other hotel bedrooms. You refuse to visit any places, when the club tries to organize it for you. That's what most players are like, then and now. As a player, I had no interest at all in the rest of the world. So Nepal seemed amazing. My eyes were opened for the first time.

Mind you, it took a bit of getting used to. I asked for a cup of tea, and it wasn't like tea as I knew it. I ordered coffee and it seemed to be made out of charcoal. All the same, I loved it. I rang Bonnie and said it's brilliant, I'm not coming back, I'm staying, so you get your visa as quick as you can and come out and join me.

They put me up at the Hilton at Katmandu, so I had fairly good mod-cons. I had a TV, which none of the players had. It was amazing waking up every morning and looking out and seeing these massive mountains. Everest wasn't far away. It was breathtaking.

I was given a car and chauffeur. The motor was fairly beat up, an old-fashioned long thing, left over from the last war. It had a flag flying at the front, because it was a government car. The chauffeur drove on his horn, pushing all the animals out of the way, and other cars and people, if they got in his way. He'd always get out of the car before me and open my door. When he was waiting for me, he'd stand polishing the bonnet and the door handles.

None of the players had cars. Some came on their bikes to training – even though they were in the national team. They lived like most of the ordinary people in Nepal, in sort of shack-type houses, with no electricity. I went to their homes once or twice and they'd ask if I'd like a cup of tea. I'd look round and see no cooker, no fridge, and wonder where the tea was coming from. They'd heat the water in a billycan over an open fire.

The chances of getting a dicky tummy were pretty high. The food was so hot and so spicy. Even at breakfast, they served you spicy stuff. I used to wake up with my arse red hot every morning, till I gave up the local food and asked for things like Corn Flakes. Then my tummy was okay. But they couldn't have been nicer. Everyone was so polite, kind and helpful.

The country was football daft. It's their big game, so miles out in the country, you'd come across little kids wearing football shirts. Tatty ones, of course, all pretty scruffy, but football kit all the same. At first sight, on arrival, I'd never realized that.

The biggest surprise, football-wise, was that they could get crowds of 80,000 in their national stadium. It wasn't expensive for them. They only paid about 50p each to get in, as it is a very poor country. When we first played there, it was absolutely packed, like sardines, up to the rafters.

It was an old wooden stadium, in terrible condition. The minute I looked up all the people, crammed in, and all the wood, I thought yeah, an accident waiting to happen here. It had tragedy written all over it. Nothing did go wrong, when I was there, but a few years later they did have a terrible fire. It was on a day when they'd locked the gates to keep people out – and also in. I think quite a few died that day.

I was coach for the national team. There was a sort of manager figure, Rupert Prakash, who had been captain of the team and was very revered. He spoke good English and so did all the players. So I had no trouble with the language, except when I was out, meeting ordinary people.

There was no professional league in Nepal. But once you got in the national squad, the government fixed you up with a good job, or they promoted you to a better job so you could have time off. The players worked in places like the post office, government offices, the police. Prakash was a police superintendent, something like that, a big job anyway. A lot of the players had been Gurkha soldiers. That's how they came to speak English, and also why they were so fit. They trained like soldiers, up and down steps, lots of running.

Each morning, when I arrived for training, they would line up, put their hands together in front of them, as if praying, and then bow before me. Not quite like the Wimbledon players. I'd say right, let's have you, let's get started. They'd then do the hands together thing again, bow once again, and then at last they'd get started.

I would say the standard of football was pretty low. About Fourth Division. One or two who played for the national team were professional, but they played abroad, in India or Pakistan. Pakistan was where most of the money was for footballers in that region. I had 28 in the squad and one helper with the training who was a fitness coach. He didn't actually know much about training, or football.

We'd train twice a day. At 6.00 in the morning, when it was still cool, till about 9.30, then I'd go back to my hotel, have a meal, have a swim or bath, or make notes, work out training schedules. Then *we'd train again in the evening when it was cool again, from 5.00 to about 7.00. Despite being so near the Himalayas, and seeing all that snow, the climate was tropical, very hot during the day.*

They didn't have much idea about coaching or tactics. When I arrived, I found they did 11-a-sides in training which were just like kids in a school playground. Everyone would rush forward when they were attacking, then all run back when they were defending. It was pure fun for them.

I said hold on, stop all this, what's going on? When you lose the ball, who's going to defend? They said oh we all rush back. I said but you're not. You're all out of position. I said look, the full back's rushed forward, and the centre half, and the whole defence, and all of them have stayed up, trying to score. It was incredible. All they wanted to do was score goals, not defend, just like kids. No one in a playground ever wants to defend or be goalie, do they?

So I said you five, you are the defence, you don't go up. If they disobeyed, or forgot, I would tell Prakash to tell them in their own language. He would give them a right bollocking. Yabba yabba yabba. I couldn't understand a word, but I could see their faces, looking scared stiff, having the fear of God put into them.

I worked out that the one with the best feet and a good touch thought he was the main goalscorer and I told him right, you are taking all set plays from now on. He went mad: 'No, I am the goalscorer. I do not take corners. I stay in the goalmouth and I score the goals.' I said oh no you don't, not any more. You are the best player in a dead ball situation, so I want you to practise corner kicks till you can land them at the near and far post, where they will be nodded in by our centre halves. They had never practised any sort of set plays before. It was normally the nearest man to the ball who played it. We had a couple of big fellas, both six-foot-three. I wanted them to come up and give us a chance of scoring a few goals. I knew we would in general play. He still protested, saying he would be out of the danger area by taking corners. I said hard luck. It's what's best for the team that's important.

He took them of course, and it worked. We managed to score a few important goals from set plays. They were quite good players, really. It was just that they had no discipline and no shape. I made them stick to their positions, not go haring off but it was tough and frustrating trying to get the message across.

In the dressing room, they were just like players everywhere. Some larking around, winding the others up, some being got at by the others. I think footballers are the same the world over. You always come across the same characters.

The team captain was the superstar and had played for Nepal for about ten years, so they all respected him. I said to him one morning, how was things, was everyone okay? He stands up in the dressing room and points to one player and says, 'All okay – except for Raj. He has spent last night shagging, and it is not good enough.' All the rest of the lads start laughing. Poor old Raj shakes his head, denying it all. 'It is not good enough, all this shagging,' repeats the captain. 'She might get baby.'

Poor Raj is getting dead embarrassed and dead worried. I don't know whether it was true or just a wind-up, but I went along with it.

'Thanks, skip,' I'd say. 'I'd better keep a close eye on young Raj from now on.'

'Oh please sir, no sir, not me sir,' Raj would say.

I think they all did have lots of girls, like footballers everywhere. Girls would be hanging around them. I'd often come across them by chance sitting in cafés, with loads of girls. They had nowhere else to go, having no money, no flats of their own, nor a car. They all lived at home, except for the ones married with kids.

There was no boozing, none that I was aware of. They couldn't afford it for a start, though I did now and again spot one in a caff with a can of beer. There were no nightclubs for people like them, no discos to go to pick up women.

There were one or two nightclubs in the big posh hotels, but they were for hotel residents, which usually meant foreigners. And there weren't many of them. In Nepal, there was no ex-pat community. I didn't meet one other Brit out there, and very few Europeans.

They were all very aware about loss of face, on or off the pitch. Someone being found drunk or caught with another woman would be in disgrace. In a small place, everyone would find out. So you didn't get that sort of faffing around we get in Britain. They took their training and their football very seriously.

And we did well. My main job was to get them through the Asian group qualification round for the 1986 World Cup. That was why they hired me.

We had a gap between matches early on, and the big man from their FA, the one who was a prince or something in their royal family, asked if I'd like to go on safari. That amazed me. I hadn't thought of there being jungles in Nepal. I'd never been on a safari. So I said yeah.

He arrives with a couple of trucks and off we go for the weekend. We went to this lake, crossed this river, and I'm watching Mount Everest all the time. We come to this grassy area, with the grass up to my head, and I thought what's going on? Then we come to these tame elephants, and get on them, climb up on top. There's a sort of driver in front, a boy who hits the elephant to direct it. I'm sitting just behind him. As he swishes his stick, I have to dodge out of the way, so he doesn't hit me on the hooter.

We wade through this river, still on the back of the elephants, and I'm looking down, seeing alligators, swimming around us. I think, if I fall off this bloody elephant, I'm a gonner. From time to time, the boy stops the elephant, makes it get down on its knees and I get off. He says it's their lunch break. They then tear up these trees and eat them. It was like a petrol stop, filling up their engines.

We set up a camp, and slept there. It was brilliant, though I was scared in the night hearing lions or whatever roaring. We had a ring of big candles round the camp to keep the animals off, but the noise of those lions, I thought Jesus, they won't be scared by a few candles.

The special thing about the area we were in was the white rhino. It's about the only place in the world that has them. There's not many, but we did eventually find one. It was a big bloody thing. Looked as if it was wearing a coat of arms, with a massive hooter. And it was, sure enough, white. He came near us, snorting away, and I thought I hope he doesn't rush us. But he went off.

We came to another river and the prince asks me if I like fish. I *said yeah, but I couldn't see any fishing tackle. His man pulls out a little stick of dynamite and throws it in the river. A minute later, there's this massive explosion. They all ran downstream and guess what, they're pulling out hundreds of fish. It's the soundwaves in the water that kills them, blasts their eardrums, that's what I was told. We had fish that night, cooked over the open fire. There was masses left, so when we came to little villages, the Prince would give them out to the locals, who were all of course thrilled. I loved going on that safari, something I had never imagined in my life I'd ever do.*

Well, back to the football. For the World Cup qualification we were in a group with some very strong teams, including Hong Kong, Korea,

Cable : ANFA   विकास – अनुशासन – गतिशिलता   Phone; 2-15703

अखिल नेपाल फूटबल संघ
All Nepal Football Association

(Affiliated to AFC & FIFA)
&
Recognised by National Sports Council, Nepal
Registration No N/06
DASHRATH RANGASHALA
TRIPURESHWOR
KATHMANDU.
NEPAL

President	Vice President		Hony. Secretary
Kamal Bahadur Thapa	Brig. Gen. Rabi Shamsher J. B. R. Retd.	Bimal prasad Srivastab	Tika Ram Shahi
	Gambhir Pradhan	D.I.G. Hang Sing Chemjong	

Ref No.   *Dated* ....

Hony. Treasure
Deependra Rimal

Training in Kathmandu Friday 13th Nov.

Travel to CALCUTTA Saturday 14th Nov.

Get aclimatised 7 days before first match

Tournament on Nov. 20 - 27th .

Heny. Joint-Secretary
Surendra Bahadur Shrestha

If possible may we have training ground away from the city.
may be a University pitch,private so we can practice our ½
SET plays & tacticts.

Total days of Training ; 4? days

Kathmandu 17 days

Birgunj 18 days

Executive Member
Purushottam Prasad Shrestha
Prakas K. C.
Devendra Bahadur Shah
Ananda Bahadur Shrestha
Deepak Bajracharya

Calcutta 7 days $+ \left(3 \ GAMES. = 14 \ DAYS \right)$
" $\underline{42 \ DAYS.}$ $-$

$\left(6 \ WEEKS + 1 \ WEEK \ CALCUTTA. \right)$

Joe's notes for his Nepal team preparing to play India, 1987.

네팔代表蹴球団

Leader
Rabi SJB Rana

Manager
Prakash K. C.

Coach
J. Kinnear

Nepal National team

Joe, with garlands, back row, 3rd from left.

Malaysia. We did a hell of a lot of travelling. We didn't have much of a chance, a little country like Nepal against much richer, bigger countries. But we did well, ending up fourth out of six in the group. Korea went through to the World Cup – Malaysia was runner-up.

I enjoyed it so much, and they seemed to like me, so later I went back for another short contract (Oct-Nov 1987) for the South Asia Federation championships, the sort of European Championships for their region. There were even stronger nations this time, with huge populations, such as India and Pakistan. We did well, amazing really, for such a small country.

We got to the final in our group and had to play India in Calcutta. Bonnie came out to India for the match. When we were at the airport in Katmandu, to fly to Calcutta, the royal prince came to see us off. It was a joke airport, just a couple of huts.

The prince is there and we all get lined up. I wore these jodhpur things, the national dress, plus green blazers. A girl comes down the line with a big bowl of flowers and petals and a bowl of some sort of dye. She puts a garland round each of our necks and a big dot on our foreheads with the dye. This was a great honour and was meant to bring us good luck. Someone thanked me afterwards for not wearing a suit and jacket. I did it to show respect.

There were about 80,000 at the match in Calcutta. We got beaten 4-3, but we did well enough. Everyone in Nepal was very pleased at how far we'd got. The Indian crowd wasn't so pleased. Our lads really got stuck in, being tough Gurkha types, and of course I made sure they were up for it.

Coaching Woodford Town had been a bit of a joke. In Nepal, it was serious. I enjoyed the coaching, the whole experience, even all the travelling. I discovered that coaching seemed to fit me like a glove.

Chapter Seventeen

I wasn't back in England for very long, after my first spell in Nepal, when I got a phone call from an agent asking if I'd fancy a job in Dubai. He had a sheikh who was looking for someone. Where on earth's Dubai? I asked. In the United Arab Emirates. I didn't even know the Arabs played football.

He said the money would be good – £50,000 a year tax free. So that sounded interesting. Then I remembered it was where Don Revie went, after he left the England job. They'd also had Carlos Alberto out there and Minotti, among other famous managers.

It so happened the sheikh was staying in Brighton. I was asked if I'd go down and talk to him. I expected some bearded bloke in flowing robes and a funny head-dress, but there he was in a three-piece suit, like any British businessman. His English was perfect. He confirmed the money, and also told me what the perks and bonuses would be. I said I'd go out for a week, see if I liked it, see if they liked me.

When I got out there, it was breathtaking. So modern and luxuri-ous, compared with Nepal, in fact compared with anywhere, with masses of country clubs, sports clubs, all equipped with the best possible facilities. I couldn't believe it. Didn't take me long to accept the job.

Unlike Nepal, there were thousands of Brits out there, all earning a bundle, rolling in it, shovelling it in. Arabs like to have a European partner when they run a business. Also a European can't do it on his own, can't own his own business, he had to be a partner with a local

Arab. It helps both sides. The Arab really owns the company, takes most of the profits, but does little work. The European runs the business, and makes a bloody good salary. So they were all happy.

It means you come across Europeans everywhere – French chefs, Italian waiters, British managers. And it means you can get French croissants or English beer everywhere. Life for these ex-pats is fantastic. Brilliant beaches, amazing golf courses. It's a fantasy world.

One of the many perks which came with my job was a five-bedroom villa, complete with cook, gardener, cleaner and chauffeur, all paid for by them. I didn't have to do a thing. The staff were Indians, cheap labour probably, in Arab terms, but pleased to be there.

SHARJAH CLUB

UNITED ARAB EMIRATES
SHARJAH

Telephone : 22558 - 373342
P. O. Box : 55

No.

Date

نادي الشارقة

دولـة الأمـارات العربيـة المتحـدة
الشـارقة

تليفـون : ٢٢٥٥٨ ، ٣٧٣٢٤٢
ص. ب : ٥٥

الرقم

التاريخ

عقد اتفاق

AGREEMENT

This 16th day of July, 1985 mutually agreed between :

A. Sharjah Sports Club & Representative
   "FIRST PARTY"

B. Mr. JOE KINNEAR
   "SECOND PARTY"

1. The Second Party has agreed to work in the capacity of Foot Ball Coach on a monthly salary of : £3000/- payable by end of each month.

2. This agreement will come into effect from 1.8.1985 provided he is available with the Club on the same date, for one year, and renewable on expiry of this period, with the same conditions, as existing in this agreement made on the above mentioned date, if either party is not interested in the renewal of the agreement, will have to give two months notice of their intention to discontinue the agreement. However, if either of the parties, not conveying any view to the other about this agreement, this will automatically be considered renewed.

Pay ✓
+ INCREASE

انه في يوم ١٩٨٠/٧/١٦م تمّ الاتفاق بين :

١) نادى الشارقة الرياضي ، وممثلـــــه /
   (طـرف اول)

ب / السيد / جـوكينيـا
   (طرف ثاني)

١) قبل الطرف الثاني العمــــل لـــــدى
   الطرف الاول بوظيفة " مدرب كـرة قدم " براتب شهري وقدره
   = /٣٠٠٠/ = استرليني تدفع نهاية كل شهر .

٢) يعمل بهذا العقد اعتبارا من ١٩٨٠/٨/١م
   بشرط تواجده بالنادي في نفس التاريخ ولمدة (عام)
   قابلة للتحديد لفترات اخرى وبنفس الشروط الواردة فيه
   اعتبارا من تاريخ التعيين ما لـم يخطـــــر
   احد الطرفين الآخر برغبته في عدم التجديد قبل نهاية
   العقد بشهرين على الاقل ، والاّ اعتبر العقد مجددا
   تلقائيـا . .

Joe goes to the United Arab Emirates as coach of Sharjah, 1985.

The club I was managing was called Sharjah. Sharjah is one of the states which make up the United Arab Emirates, with a population of about 40,000. It's on the coast, about half an hour's drive from Dubai, which is the main state, next door, with the main city, and a much bigger population. I think the total population of the whole country is about one million – but a lot of them live out in the desert. Sharjah was in their top division – well, they only have one division. It was owned by Sheikh Abdullah. But the three Dubai clubs dominated their league.

There were no foreign players out there – they all had to be locals. And there were no transfers – you play for the club of the area where you were born. So all the players playing for Sharjah were born in Sharjah.

The Dubai clubs had more players to choose from, being a much bigger place, so that's one reason why they did so well. But the main reason was money. Their clubs were owned by the top sheikhs so they were made. But there was intense rivalry because the three Dubai clubs were owned by the three brothers of the ruling family. They had a club each.

Our sheikh in Sharjah was pretty wealthy, as that's where the oil is, on the coast. But there were also sheikhs who were not so wealthy. We were competing at the top with the Dubai clubs, but below us was a huge gap. A bit like the Scottish League. We were, say, Aberdeen and they were like Rangers and Celtic. We'd go to some places, driving in our luxury coach across the desert for three hours, seeing nothing at all except camels or herdsmen, stuff the local team 9-0, then drive back.

All the players were technically amateur. They didn't get paid for playing, but in the end they did. As in Nepal, they all supposedly had jobs, in the police, customs, but they could get endless time off for training.

They didn't just get a good job when they joined the club, they also got a good house. The players lived in luxury villas, practically at the club, like a high-class Olympic village. The facilities at the club included an Olympic-size swimming pool, indoor five-a-side pitches, basketball courts. It was actually a sports club, so there was more than just football being played, but football was the main thing. We had 10 training pitches for football, all immaculate. Anything we wanted, we just asked for. Money was no problem.

I was the manager-coach. I inherited four trainers but they hadn't been properly trained. It's funny how they don't have Arab managers, even now, when their football is so developed. Some of their players are national heroes, but don't become managers. I think it's because it's all so friendly, people being related, all living together. They find it hard to manage people they know so well, to bollock them, drop them. They can't do it. That's why the place is full of foreign managers, like Yugoslavians, who are very tough.

At Sharjah, there were 100 players, but that was because we ran so many teams, from the age of eight upwards. In the senior squad I had 32 players whom I worked with.

They were much better, more skilful than the Nepali players, and they should have been, with all those facilities. They were probably our present Second Division level. They had great skill and could juggle with the ball all day. They hated any physical contact. In Nepal, they could get stuck in, be physical. The Arabs don't like that.

I was amazed the first day I took training when I suddenly heard this cry going up, 'Allahu Akbar, Allahu Akbar'. Then they all got out prayer mats, moved against this wall, got down on the mats and started praying and chanting. I think it means 'God is great'. It happened all the time, in the middle of training or in matches at half-time. About three times every day they're at it.

Before kick-off in each game they got into a huddle, locked arms, bending over, with the ball in the middle. I'd never seen that done before. Now it's quite common.

The stadium was brilliant and the crowds fairly good – about 10,000 for an ordinary league match – 25,000 for a cup final. Football is their main sport. UAE did after all qualify for the 1990 World Cup finals.

The players showed utter respect – no discipline problems at all. But they didn't show a lot of emotion, so it was hard to know what they were really thinking. They could understand English, but spoke Arabic amongst themselves. When I told them something, they'd say

'Yes, Captain'. They'd say 'Inshallah' a lot. God be with you.

In Nepal, they were more open with you, keener in a way, but then they needed more help, being a poor country, with their players living ordinary lives. You could get them to throw themselves around, go for death and glory. With the Arabs, they were too well looked after, nice house, nice job for life. There wasn't a lot of pressure on them to knock themselves out.

If you wanted something, you'd go to your sheikh. Say you're getting married, want money for the wedding, a player would go to the sheikh and he would get the money. The sheikhs had oil money coming out of their ears at the time.

Even the supporters had big fancy black limos. If we'd done well, won a match against one of the Dubai teams, they'd roar through the streets of Sharjah firing their Kalashnikovs in the air. Real rifles, real bullets. They'd just let rip, firing up in the air. I was fucking frightened, when I first saw it. I thought if that's them celebrating, what the hell do they do when we get stuffed ...

There was no problem getting a drink. Dubai is not like Oman and Qatar. Dubai is like New York or any European city – pubs and clubs at every corner. Ex-pats from the other Arab states come into Dubai at the weekend to get blitzed.

The Arabs of course are not supposed to drink, and they don't really. I went into a few of their homes, saw one or two have the odd beer, in the privacy of their homes, but they wouldn't do it in public.

A lot of my players, and players from the other big clubs, would go off to London in the off-season and spend all their money living it up, in the clubs, letting their hair down, doing the sort of stuff they wouldn't do at home.

I managed Sharjah for two seasons. We never won the league but we were in the top three each season.

Then coming home one summer, in 1987, I met Dave Mackay on the plane to London. He'd been coaching in Qatar. He said he'd been offered a job in Dubai, with one of the top teams, Al Shabab, a much richer club than the one I was at. It's owned by Sheikh Mohammed, who's the biggest racehorse owner in the world.

Dave didn't know whether to take it or not. He asked me if he took it, whether I'd come with him. And that's what happened. Dave became manager and I was coach. I got £75,000 a year, tax free.

There was more expectation with Al Shabab than with Sharjah, so there was more pressure. The rivalry between the Dubai clubs was very intense, which you were soon aware of. We finished third at the end of the season – and my contract was over. We'd only signed for one year.

I enjoyed my three years with the Arabs. I only had good experiences there. The social life was brilliant, the facilities amazing, the country clubs incredible, the climate great. There was a bit of the gin and tonic ex-pat brigade in the posher clubs, who thought they were superior, but they didn't bother me. I think Bonnie enjoyed it as well, though she wasn't there full time.

On the football side, it helped me to learn my trade. It gave me an insight into handling a large squad, how to delegate, how to work out training schedules, keep everyone occupied. And the fact that there were no transfers meant you didn't have to travel round all the time scouting. So, I was very grateful for the experience.

Chapter Eighteen

So how was it for you? That's what I asked Bonnie. Hard enough being a player's wife, subsuming your life under their life, even if in theory they do come home in the afternoon and have nothing else to do except watch children's programmes on television. But being married to a coach or manager, one trying to get started, that must be like being a foreign mercenary's wife, with a partner liable to rush off around the world in search of work. What do you do? Stay at home and take up knitting, good works or what?

'Oh I wanted to join Joe. After a week out in Nepal on his own, when he rang up and said come out quick, I was very excited. The journey wasn't much fun, though, travelling all on my own, and it took forever.

'Arriving in Katmandu was amazing. Just 24 hours earlier I'd been in the heart of London, and now I was in a field with a few cows and a shed in the middle of nowhere. This was the airport. And no sign of Joe. Yes, typical, he wasn't there. They'd gone off to play in Korea or somewhere and got stuck.

'But there was a government official there, with a car and driver. He said he was going to take me to my hotel, but first would I like a tour of Katmandu. I said yes. It was mesmerizing, spellbinding, like going back in time to the middle ages.

'We got to the hotel, I checked in, unpacked, got into bed, fell asleep – then Joe rang to say don't unpack, we're moving to another hotel, we're going to the Sheraton.

'I stayed in Nepal a month – and I loved it all. While Joe was training or playing or travelling, I explored the country with our driver. I roamed everywhere, going to the 11th-century villages, meeting the locals. They are such happy, friendly people.

'After a month, I had to get back for the children. They were getting older by now, late teenagers, so there wasn't the same worry about them. I did have someone living in, but I decided I had to go and see how they were getting on.

'By the time Joe went to Dubai, the kids had left school, so I could stay with Joe longer. He went ahead first, as in Nepal, in August I think, then I joined him in September. I stayed till Xmas, then came home to see how the kids were. I loved it, just as much as Nepal, though in a different way. Nepal was historically and culturally fascinating. Dubai was decadent, in a way, being so modern and luxurious.

'In the second year, I again went out for several months at a time, and still liked it, all the luxury, all the facilities, but I was becoming a bit bored with nothing much to do. So I found a little job. I did exhibitions and promotions for a tobacco firm. We'd drive out to some remote village, go to the village shop, do a little display, then give out gawdy T-shirts and sunglasses to all the people. Most of the village people didn't smoke, but they liked the T-shirts.

'I'd been warned, as a woman, never to drive on my own, so I always drove with my girlfriend, whom I worked with. One day we got cut up by this Arab driver, who swerved in front of us. He got out and was very abusive, shouting at us. My friend said on no account get out – sit still, say nothing. She knew the Arabs. They can be very chauvinistic. So we drove off, but found he was following us. It was very scary.

'In the end we stopped. I got out and said do you know whose car this is? I told him the name of the sheikh Joe worked for. That settled him. He got scared and drove off. But it was a bit frightening at the time.

'When Joe decided to come home, I was heartbroken, I really was. Many ex-pat wives hate it out there, can't stand it, despite all the facilities, all the luxuries. You see marriages collapsing all the time because the woman is homesick. That never happened to me. I found it all fascinating.

'But of course I didn't know what sort of work Joe was coming back to, or what sort of life we would be going to lead next.'

Chapter Nineteen

Because of all the foreign jobs I'd got rid of the pub by then. I'd decided I really did want to make a go of being a football coach. But I didn't know what job I'd be able to find, or where.

I can't remember how long I spent hanging around, perhaps just a few weeks, till one day in 1987 I got a call from Dave Mackay again. He'd been offered the managership of Doncaster Rovers. Dave Cussack had been sacked.

I didn't really fancy it. They were almost at the bottom of the Fourth Division and sounded in bad nick. But Dave persuaded me to join him. He said it would get me back on the English circuit. After thinking about it for a while, I agreed to be his assistant manager. The money was poor, less than half what I'd been getting in Dubai. And that was all tax free. I got £22,000 and I think Dave, as manager, was on £35,000.

Having agreed, we thought we'd do the job properly, so me and Bonnie decided to move up there. We rented out our London house to a Japanese bank manager, and went to look for something up there. I was new of course to Doncaster, never lived in the North before, didn't know what's what – which is the nice bits and the not so nice – but we saw this converted stable block, a few miles away at Bawtry, which looked okay. The bloke wanted £32,000 for it. I said I'm the new man at Rovers, by the way, trying to get the price down. He said oh-aye. Not at all impressed. But I did get him down to £28,000 and bought it.

I never did see any rich areas of Doncaster itself. I suppose there must be some. I only saw the bits round the ground. It all seemed to be fish and chip shops, mushy peas, blokes in cloth caps on the terraces drinking Bovril. And not many of them. I think the gates were about 1,200. My first impression was that it all looked pretty depressing, coming from Dubai. But the people were warm, very friendly.

The club had no money of course. In pre-season, we couldn't afford to go on any sort of tour, or play against any half-decent club. All we could manage was a game against a miners' team from a local colliery. The club was in turmoil, with huge debts, though we didn't know the half of it when we arrived.

What Doncaster gave me was an insight into scouting in the lower leagues. The club couldn't afford any transfer fees, and nobody in a first team would want to come to us anyway, so we had to concentrate on scouting the reserve and junior teams of the big northern clubs, the ones near us, like Leeds, Sheffield, even Rotherham.

What we had to do was spot the ones with potential, who weren't making it so far. He might fancy coming to us, as he wouldn't have to move house. I'd go and see him and promise him first-team exposure. That's how Doncaster and clubs like it survived, and still do. That's how they picked up Brian Deane from Leeds and Rufus Brevett from Derby, and Mark Rankine and quite a few others, all for nothing, on free transfers.

Our biggest proper signing, for money, was Les Robinson from Chesterfield. He's now captain of Oxford. We paid £16,000 for him from Stockport. Seemed a fortune at the time, for Doncaster.

We had, of course, the impression that there would be more money available but it didn't seem to be there. Dave began to get disillusioned. After about a season and a half, he got fed up and resigned.

I was asked to stay on, as manager, for the rest of the season. I wasn't given a contract, but I was told if I could keep them in the division, they'd give me a two-year contract. I can't believe I was so

Doncaster Rovers Football Club Ltd

BELLE VUE, DONCASTER DN4 5HT
Telephone: (0302) 539441/2/3

Vice-President: K. JACKSON
Vice-President: R. JONES
Chairman: B. BOLDRY
Vice-Chairman: M. COLLETT
Directors: T. HAMILTON
P. WETZEL
J. BURKE
K. CHAPPELL
M. O'HORAN
W. TURNER
Manager: J. KINNEAR
Secretary: J. OLDALE
Reserve/
Youth Coach: S. BEAGLEHOLE
Physiotherapist: G. DELAHUNT
Honorary W. ERSKINE
Club Doctors: C. HEAD

HONOURS

3rd Division Champions (North)
1934-35; 1946-47; 1949-50

4th Division Champions
1965-66; 1968-69

Winners - Sheffield County Cup
1890-91; 1911-12; 1935-36; 1937-38;
1955-56; 1967-68; 1975-76; 1985-86

North Midland League Champions
1967

Midland Counties League Champions
1896-97; 1898-99

Northern Intermediate League Cup
1984-85 1986-87

The official Club Photographer is Roy Ingram
Danum Press Agency - Tel: Doncaster 60475

The opinions expressed in this programme are those
of the contributors and do not necessarily reflect the
opinions of the Board of Directors and Management
of Doncaster Rovers Football Club Ltd.

JOE KINNEAR
COMMENTS

Firstly, I would like to thank the Board for showing their faith in me as new Manager for the Club.

I know I have a difficult task ahead, but I feel there is a great potential of supporters in Doncaster and it is up to me to get the team right and bring success to the town. It's what the town deserves.

It has been a very hectic week and I am very pleased to have signed Vince Brockie who I know has a very bright future and is an excellent acquisition for the club. I am sorry to lose Paul Raven but wish him every success with West Bromwich Albion. He deserved this improvement in his career. Although we have been offered 6 figure transfer fees for other young players we have held on to them.

Finally, I would hope that the supporters will show me the same good faith as the Board and that we can all start to look forward and not backward. I take this opportunity of welcoming Chris Turner, Manager of Cambridge United, their officials, players and supporters to tonight's match.

Enjoy the match.

Doncaster v. Cambridge. Monday March 27, 1989:
Joe takes over as manager.

gullible. I didn't get anything written down. I just believed what they said.

I was also pretty naïve when it came to selling players. If the club did find anyone good, we had of course to sell them, to balance the books. We decided to sell Brian Deane. He'd done well for us, but we needed the money. Sheffield United were interested and asked how much. I valued him at £75,000. They went to tribunal and after a lot of argument, we ended up having to sell him for £16,000. That was nothing then, and bugger all now, when you think he was later worth millions. I valued him on his potential, saying he was still a young lad who would get better, but the tribunal saw no reason to think he would do better. So that was it. The chairman was desperate for money. I shouldn't have let it get to the tribunal but done a deal. To make matters worse, only half of the £16,000 was paid up front, and I didn't see a penny of it to spend on the team. It just went into the club, to pay its debts.

However, I managed to keep the club up and went off on holiday with Bonnie in the summer. I came back for pre-season a bit early, getting ready to play various local miners' teams.

When I arrived, I met the club secretary. He says oh, we've been trying to get hold of you all summer, we didn't know where you were. 'What's happened?' I said. 'We've been taken over,' he said. 'New people have come in, the old lot of directors have gone, it's all new round here ...'

I went into my office, the manager's office, and there was Billy Bremner, sitting at my desk. It wasn't his fault, of course. The new lot had decided to bring him in, part of their new look for the club. He was a legend after all. He'd been sacked as manager of Leeds, but he was still a legend. I thought he was off his head, coming to Doncaster, after managing Leeds, but there he was. He was all apologetic. But there was nothing he could do.

The new lot, some new syndicate who'd taken over, knew nothing about the promise the old lot had made to me. I'd got nothing in writing. There was no money anyway. Everyone was skint. I understood all that, but it was all very badly handled. The upshot was I got

114

six months' salary in my hand, about £15,000, as I'd got an increase when Dave Mackay left. They gave me the money and said cheerio, all the best.

The only good thing that happened during those two years at Doncaster was the house I'd bought, the one I'd paid £28,000 for. When I came to sell it, I got £65,000. I was out of work, but I did get something out of Doncaster.

Chapter Twenty

As we got near the end of 1999, there was still nothing happening on the job front for Joe. Even the rumours and newspaper speculation about his being on the list for various places was drying up. At Blackburn, Tony Parkes, once again, had stepped into the gap as caretaker manager and was doing well, though one paper had a quote from Bertie Vogts, the former coach of the German national team, saying he was interested in applying for the Blackburn job. He had been a member of Germany's World Cup-winning team in 1974 and as the national team manager had won the European Championships held in England in 1996. If it came to showing us your medals, even Joe could not quite compete with Bertie.

There had been rumours that John Gregory was still under pressure but no contact had been made. On the radio, on the way to see Joe one day, I heard a report that Deadly Doug had allegedly offered £3 million for two young Peterborough players, one called Simon Davies – the other's name I hadn't caught.

When I told Joe, he knew at once both players. The other must be Matthew Etherington, he said. They were both good prospects. He had checked them out while at Wimbledon.

So what have you been doing Joe, I asked, since I saw you last week? Norralot, he said, let me think.

On Tuesday, they'd had Nicholas for the day, their two-year-old grandson, the light of Bonnie's life, and of Joe's. Joe had played with Nicholas in their house and garden, then they'd taken him to Golders Hill Park, to look at the animals, play on the swings.

Nice family fun, something more managers should make time for in their lives, but not exactly what Joe was looking for at that moment, aged only 52, with another decade in football ahead of him, so he hoped, before he retired. He was now convinced he was fit and well enough to get back to real work.

Anything else this last week, any other excitements to share?

'Well, yesterday was a bit livelier,' he said. 'I was sitting around here at ten in the morning, not knowing what to do with myself, when the phone rang and it was Jonah ...'

Jonah Lomu, the great New Zealand rugby player? He was currently in the news as he might be joining an English rugby club.

'No, Vinnie Jones. Jonah's his nickname at Wimbledon. Gawd knows where it comes from. Anyway he says, "What you doing gaffer?" I says nuffink. He says how about going racing at Newmarket with me. I can come and pick you up in my car. So I says fine, great.

'He only lives a few miles north of me, in Herts. He has a farm, deep in the countryside, with lots of dogs and animals. So it was roughly on his way, picking me up.

'I'm in Vinnie's car when his car phone goes. It's the director of the film he's working on, a bloke called Guy Ritchie, saying he wants Vinnie to come for a photo call. Vinnie has to have his photo taken with Brad Pitt. He's the star of the film Vinnie's working on. Vinnie says fucking hell, this is my day off, I'm going racing. Guy says it's very important. It's for *Vanity Fair*. They've been promised the cover, with Brad and Vinnie together. So Vinnie says okay then.

'He turns to me and says sorry about that, gaffer. I'll drive you home if you like, or you can come to the photo shoot. It probably won't take more than an hour. We'll still go to Newmarket, though we might miss the first race.

'I said yeah, no problem. I'll come with you. What else have I got to do?

'We drive to Streatham where I was expecting some little photographic studio. Blow me, it's only this monster set for the film they're working on. They've recreated this massive night-club, like Ceasar's Palace, and set up a full-size boxing ring. Round the ring, seated at tables, is about every bouncer and hoodlum and gangster in London. Well, that's how they looked. All massive, with tattoes and broken noses.

'In this 'ere film, Brad Pitt is playing some little Irish gypsy boy who's a brilliant bare-fisted boxer. He's all unshaven, with a little beard thing, and tattoos. Vinnie is a hard man. He spends most of the film with a bullet lodged in his front teeth.

'They were still in the middle of a scene, so me and Vinnie had to hang around, with Vinnie apologizing to me all the time. I said don't worry, I'm enjoying it. I'd never been on a film set before. They did this little scene about 20 times, with Brad Pitt having a fag taken out of his mouth. He didn't take the fag out the right way, then his cap fell off, anyway it went on and on and on. But I found it all very interesting.

'When they finally finished the scene, Brad is told about the picture with Vinnie for *Vanity Fair*. He says no way. He's not being photographed for *Vanity Fair*, not looking like this. He'll do it on Friday, when he's shaved off his stubble.

'Well, Vinnie is effing and blinding, saying why the fuck hadn't someone found out all this, before dragging him in on his day off.

'We gets to Newmarket at last, have a good day, win a few bob. On the way home, Vinnie's mobile goes and it's Guy again, the director. He says would Vinnie like to come for a drink this evening, to say farewell to Guy's girlfriend, who's going back to America. Vinnie says yeah, okay, but can he bring the gaffer. Guy says of course. I had nothing to do, had I. So I says yeah, I'll go with you.

'The party was in something called the Circus Bar in Soho. Guess who Guy's girlfriend turns out to be? It's only Madonna, innit.

'There were about 30 paparazzi outside, trying to catch people coming in. Kate Moss was there, Stella McCartney, loads of fashion and film people, half of *Who's Who*, though I didn't know most of them. What surprised me was how many actors knew me, who turned out to be football nuts. They kept on coming up at the party and saying I hope you get the Blackburn job, Joe.

'Madonna said hello to me, and was very nice, but no, I don't think she knew who I was. I talked quite a bit to Guy Ritchie about Vinnie, asked him how Vinnie was doing.

'Guy was the director of Vinnie's first film, *Lock, Stock and Two Smoking Barrels*. I think it cost only a few million or so to make, but it's earned about £200 million, something like that. The film they're now working on with Brad Pitt is called *Snatch*. The title might have changed by now. Anyway, he says Vinnie's a natural. "The camera is in love with Vinnie," he says. "The camera is very kind to Vinnie. Some people it doesn't like, and you can't do a thing about it, but Vinnie comes alive on the screen."

'It's still a secret, but one film he says he may want to do is a football film. Set in a prison. A bit like that American film a few years ago, when these American football stars get locked up, and they have a prison team against another team. Vinnie will be the one locked up, who then gets persuaded to run the prison football team, as he's been a footballer. Which happens of course, in real life. Tony Adams was in prison wasn't he. And Rixy's just out.

'If they ever make it, I might be a football consultant. Help them on the coaching side, show them what professional coaching sessions are like. It might be good fun ...'

So, quite an interesting day, for an out of work, middle-aged gent. And there was me, feeling a bit sorry for Joe, with nothing happening in his life.

PART THREE

Wimbledon

Chapter Twenty-one

Wimbledon Football Club gives football a good name. Not necessarily for its fine football, as they have had to do their share of clogging over the years, but for what they have done, giving hope to us all, inside and outside football. The pessimists think it can never happen again, what Wimbledon did, because the gap between rich and poor is now so enormous, and widening all the time. But this is to forget that even at the time, when Wimbledon performed their heroics, people said it couldn't be done, they'll blow up soon, disappear back to where they came from. Wherever that was.

A corner of the south-west suburbs of London, that's where, a suburb known for only one thing, tennis, until relatively recently. The football club was formed in 1889, old boys from a local school, but they were a non-league, amateur team until 1964 – a pretty decent amateur team because in 1963 they got to Wembley and won the FA Amateur Cup.

They didn't get into the Football League till 1977, joining the old Fourth Division. For five seasons they marked time, going up and down, up and down, then in the 1982-83 season, they suddenly got into gear, their act came together under Dave Bassett, and in four years, they zoomed up from the Fourth to the First Division, arriving in 1986, to the amazement of all. They had no stars, no money, no football history to speak of and their ground, Plough Lane, a name which suggests rough-hewn manual labour, held a maximum of only 13,000. How could they survive?

The answer is Samir Hammam, commonly known as Sam Hammam. His arrival in London happened to coincide with the birth of Wimbledon's Football League life in 1977.

Sam Hamman is a Lebanese gentleman, born in July 1947, in Dhour Shweir, up in the mountains, about a 45-minute drive from Beirut. His father was a doctor. 'My first language is Arabic, but at school I learned English and studied English history and culture. I should think I learned as much about Shakespeare at school as a boy at Eton would have done. The Lebanese education is superb.'

At university, however, Sam studied civil engineering. His first job was in Abu Dhabi, working on a new airport. Then he worked on building projects in Dubai and Sharjah – where Joe was later to work – and Saudi Arabia. The region was seeing the first flush of oil riches, with massive and expensive constructions going up, so he was in a good position as a qualified civil engineer who happened to be an Arab. It didn't matter that he was a Christian Arab, who had attended a Protestant School.

In 1972, along with two partners, he started an engineering and construction company which soon had projects all over the Middle East and in the USA. At their height, they were working on projects employing some 4,000 people in several countries.

In 1971, he had married Nada, also from Beirut, from a similar Christian Lebanese family. Their first child, Dina, a girl, was born in Beirut in 1973. Their second, a son called Zayd, was born in Dubai in 1976. When his wife was pregnant with their third child in 1977, Lebanon was being torn apart by civil war. She decided therefore to have the baby in London.

Sam had no connection with London, business or otherwise, though while at university he had done three months' work experience in a London firm of engineers. The connection was purely through his wife's sister who had fled to London from Lebanon, during the war, with her husband and children. She recommended a good maternity hospital, St Theresa's (now no more), for her sister Nada, as it was near where they lived. In Wimbledon.

Sam was working a lot in the USA, but he arrived in London in time for the birth of their third child – a daughter, Samar, the feminine of Samir.

'No, I didn't see her born. I was in the next room. Why should I watch? It is a Western thing, making a big deal out of the birth of a baby by sending the father to classes. There are highly qualified doctors around. No need for the father to be there. It is a natural thing.'

During that week he was in Wimbledon, in September 1977, living at his sister-in-law's, he went by taxi each day to visit his wife and baby in hospital. The driver was a football fan, a follower of Chelsea, who during the journey talked about football. Sam had never played it, never watched it, knew nothing about it, not even the names of the leading clubs.

'In passing, the driver mentioned that there was a little local club in Wimbledon which had just arrived in the Football League. They had no money, he said, and probably wouldn't last long. And nobody would buy them because they were worth nothing.

'This was new to me – that a football club could be bought. I had assumed that clubs were not owned by anyone, but were in common ownership, owned by the supporters or the local town.

'I think I spoke to the taxi driver on the Saturday and on Monday, I rang the club and asked to speak to the manager. I had assumed the word "manager" meant something like managing director, who managed all the affairs of the clubs. I didn't realize that in England manager means coach. So I was passed to the chairman.

'I went to see him and asked if he had any shares to sell. "How many do you want?" he said. I made an offer for 70 per cent of his shares. It was all done in about three days. I always work quickly, that has been my training in engineering. When you start a new project, you have to move fast, read the documents, get the lawyers working, estimate the cost, make the offer before anyone else does. It's then either accepted or not. But by then you are off, thinking about the next project. But my offer was accepted. On 15 September 1977, I became owner of the club.'

So how much did it cost? A figure of £600,000 has often been mentioned, but Sam shook his head. Much less, he said. I threw various figures at him, till we settled on £50,000 as his original investment. For a rich man, a relatively minor expenditure. All the same, why? Was it a romantic gesture? Had he fallen in love with the idea of this small club amongst the giants?

'It was more like a souvenir of my week in London. You do that on your travels. You see something and buy it, as a memento.

'In my business and personal life, I am not a spendthrift. I live very modestly. I have an ordinary car and I mostly travel economy. I make sure I always get value for money. I allow no one to overspend. But now and again, I buy things as a sort of hobby, like I have done it. Buying Wimbledon was like that. A spur of the moment impulse buy which I thought might be amusing.'

Did you also think it might be a good investment?

'Never. That did not enter my head. Nobody wanted to buy it, which was why nobody else had come along. You were not really buying anything, when you bought Wimbledon. No one can say I bought Wimbledon to make money.'

For the next 14 months, he disappeared, never came to London, never watched a game. He didn't even find out their results till days later as he hadn't realized you could get them on the BBC World Service.

By this time he and his family had all moved to New Jersey, in the USA, which was where most of his construction work was then taking place. His older children had started schools in the USA. But in 1979, Wimbledon ran into various financial and other difficulties. Ron Noades, the chairman, had left for Crystal Palace and Sam was being rung up all the time with problems.

He needed to make flying visits which became longer and longer. He found himself caught up in the life of the club, going to watch training, travelling to away matches. The manager,

126

Dario Gradi, had been appointed in 1978, while Sam was still an absentee owner.

'It was Dario who was my teacher, who told me about football. It was from him I learned that the most vital thing with any club, especially a club like Wimbledon, is their youth policy. That was Dario's background, working with young players rather than full professionals. I allied this with my policy of prudence. Only buy when you have the money to buy, which in our case means building up players you can sell. But not selling players until you know they can be replaced. Dario and I worked that out together as innocents, learning as we went along.'

By 1985 he had moved to England full time, followed by his family, buying a house near Regents Park. His three children went to the nearby American school in London and in due course to American universities. Gradually, Sam ran down his engineering business, becoming involved full time with Wimbledon from the early 90s, not just as managing director, but living and breathing the team, as if intoxicated by the smell of the liniment, the roar of the crowd.

On match days, he didn't sit in the stand, in the directors' box like the normal chairman, or even stick to the dug-out with the manager and coaches. He stood or ran along the touch like a demented fan, a clothed streaker who had just wandered in, not part of the club, jumping up and down, waving his hands, clutching his head. A sight which became familiar to all football fans.

Dario Gradi left in 1981, to go to Crystal Palace, and Dave Bassett, who had played for the club, was made manager.

'Dave was outstanding, and such a character, such a playful character. We suited each other. He took us to 6th in the First Division, then he thought he had gone as far as he could with Wimbledon. I didn't want him to leave, but he did, going to Watford. He had a good chairman in Elton John and a club he thought would have more money to spend and would win things.'

Bobby Gould was the next manager in 1987, again another family appointment, in that he had played for Wimbledon.

'Bobby was another excellent manager. He got us to 7th in the

League and we won the Cup Final of 1988, beating Liverpool. That was a result no one expected.

'Bobby was our first professional manager. Dario and Dave Bassett had not been managers before. But Bobby followed the systems we had set down. We make them into Wimbledon managers – they don't change Wimbledon.'

So what is a Wimbledon manager?

'Leader of the Crazy Gang of course. Dave Bassett established the gung-ho image, the rough and ready, but I established the notion of the Crazy Gang.

'When I arrived, there had been some talk of calling ourselves the Wombles, which I never liked. I don't like the Dons either. I took the Crazy Gang idea from America. There was this character who advertised on TV in New York called Crazy Eddie. Each week he would say nobody in the US could beat him for prices. If you found the same item elsewhere at a cheaper price, he would not just match it, he would give a discount. "It's not crazy," he'd shout. "It's insane!"

'I liked his character so much I decided to borrow the idea for Wimbledon. It was some years later I was told there had been a Crazy Gang on the London stage, many years earlier, before I'd ever been to England.

'I am not crazy myself. I am very careful, patient, meticulous, very serious. But I like crazy people ...'

Chapter Twenty-two

I don't know how long I was out of work after Doncaster – proba-bly just a few weeks I think, some time in September 1989 – when I got a call from Bobby Gould at Wimbledon. I didn't know him really, as our careers hadn't crossed, but I had met him at various football functions. He wanted me to be reserve team coach. David Kemp was his number two, the assistant manager. I think I started on £15,000 a year. It then went up the next year to £18,600.

Wimbledon were still at Plough Lane at the time but we trained on a public park. It was five or six pitches or so beside the main road, the A3, near Richmond Park. Richardson Evans Playing Field, that was its name. Dunno who he was. Some bloke who had left the pitches to the borough.

It had a transport caff as part of it – that was where all the play-ers used to eat after training. But anyone who used the pitches ate there as well, along with all the lorry drivers.

On certain days, you could get schools and ordinary clubs. You know the sort: 'Dog and Duck, pitch 3. The Red Lion, pitch 4. Wimbledon FC, pitches 4 and 5.'

After training, we'd go into the greasy spoon. Yet we were a First Division club, which had recently won the FA Cup. It was amazing, but nobody complained. It was part of the Crazy Gang atmosphere. Our full-time professional players would turn up for training looking just as scruffy as the Dog and Duck. You couldn't tell which were the ragged arse-ends and which were the top professionals.

Still Crazy

Wimbledon Football Club Ltd

49 Durnsford Road, Wimbledon SW19 8HG   Telephone 081-946 6311

Mr. Joe Kinnear   17 September 1990
34 Northiam
Woodside Park
Totteridge
London   N.12

Dear Mr. Kinnear

I refer to your meeting with the Team Manager, Mr. Ray Harford, and
confirm the following details regarding your position as Reserve
Team Coach of Wimbledon Football Club:

1.JOB TITLE
Reserve Team Coach

2.REMUNERATION
Basic salary, £18,600 per annum paid monthly in arrears.

3.AGREEMENT
Your appointment shall continue from the date of commencement of
employment from year to year unless terminated by either you, or
ourselves, giving to the other no less than one months notice in
writing, except in the case of gross misconduct or dereliction of
your duties, in which case the Company shall be entitled to
terminate you employment without notice or salary in lieu.

Your previous period of employment from 2 October, 1989, counts
towards Statutory Continuous Employment.

4.WORKING HOURS
Whilst you will be expected to work whatever hours are required
to properly perform the duties of a Reserve Team Coach, you may
be requested to work whatever hours are reasonably requested by
the Club as communicated to you by the Team Manager or Chief
Executive.

5.SICKNESS
You will be entitled to sick pay and leave as provided for by the
Statutory Sick Pay procedure, details of which are provided
separately and a copy of which is available for your inspection
at any time on request to the Chief Executive.

6.ANNUAL HOLIDAYS
You are entitled to 20 working days holiday each year, commencing
1 June, to be taken at any time convenient to yourself and by
arrangement with the Team Manager or Chief Executive.   Any
holiday not taken is to be carried forward to the following year
only and not without written approval of the Team Manager or
Chief Executive.

Directors: SG Reed Chairman. JH Lelliott Deputy. SGN Hammam Managing Director. Peter Cork. PR Cooper. NJD Hammam

VAT No. 561 8923 18   Registered in England   Company Registered No. 811820

Joe confirmed as reserve team coach at Wimbledon, 1990.

130

It was hell to park because of all the huge lorries. Then when you sat down for tea and a bun afterwards, there would always be a big lorry driver at the next table who would say, 'You was fucking rubbish last week against Arsenal.' Some were long-distance lorry drivers, from up North, so they'd lean over and tell us that Leeds were going to hammer us next week. It was a laugh, though.

When Bobby Gould left, Ray Harford took over as manager, and he made me his number two. I remember when we played Spurs at home (23 February 1991), Ray told me he was letting me give the team-talk. As we were playing my old team, he reckoned I'd wind the lads up, wanting to beat them. He also said I would be speaking to the press afterwards. That was something I'd never done before.

Terry Venables was the Spurs manager, and they had Lineker in the team, but of course I told our lads we would beat them, we had to beat them, it was vital for me to really get into them, show what we could do. And the lads did. They beat Spurs 5-1. An amazing day. I had a smile on my face all the time I talked to the press afterwards.

Ray then left, to become number two to Kenny Dalgish at Blackburn. I thought then I might have a chance of being manager. There were some good players coming through I'd personally worked with in the reserves – Chris Perry, Sullivan, Ardley, Dean Blackwell. I thought that would be in my favour.

I don't know who else was in for it. I don't know what was going on behind the scenes. You'll have to ask Sam. In the papers, it was being predicted that I would get the job, then one paper had a story that Phil Neal had been offered it and turned it down. The usual round of rumours.

I don't know if it was true or not, but I gather that Doug Ellis, chairman of Aston Villa, spoke to Sam. He said they had a very good youth team coach who was going places. They should give him a chance to be manager – this was Peter Withe. He got the job.

It was a terrible shock to me. He brought in Mick Buxton from Scunthorpe as his number two. I was demoted to number three. You have to accept that in football, new managers bring in their own people. But I did think of leaving. I could see no future for me, now I'd been put back.

I talked to Sam and he said I still had plenty to learn in management. I had to keep at it – and all that crap. I was hurt because I felt I'd done enough to justify being given a chance. I decided I'd stay a year, see how it went, then start applying elsewhere. I had never applied anywhere else. Still haven't.

Peter Withe   took one look at our lot, the Crazy Gang, and was pretty horrified by what he saw. He thought they were all scruffy, which they were. I think it was a bit of a culture shock for him, coming to our scruffy training ground with the Dog and Duck on the next pitch, the transport caff with the lorry drivers, compared to playing for England or Aston Villa with all their great facilities.

He said that jeans were out. He didn't want to see anyone turning up for training in jeans or T-shirts. And he didn't like long hair or beards. They had to go as well. And on match days, it had to be blazers, collars and ties, the full smart stuff.

Well, being Wimbledon, that didn't go down well. They all did the opposite, didn't they. On the pitch, or in actual training, I couldn't fault them. No team worked harder on their football. But off the pitch, well they hadn't been used to being bossed around. If you had said to them no T-shirts, then the next day, all 20 would have turned up in identical scruffy T-shirts. That's the way their minds worked. You'd say no beards – and none of them would shave for two weeks. Their attitude was 'I'll do and wear what I like'.

Peter also fell out with several important players, who got put back in the reserves. There were some strong characters at Wimbledon – Laurie Sanchez, Alan Cork, big personalities, who knew how to wind you up. But they were also good pros. Being put back in the reserves made them pretty fed up.

But the biggest thing was that the team didn't play well. I think when Peter arrived we were 7th in the league. By about halfway through the season, we'd dropped to 17th. I had nothing against Peter though some of the players seemed to. I just got on with the training.

Anyway, in January 1992 he got sacked. On the motorway, Sam

sacked him, that's what I heard. I was made caretaker manager till the end of the season.

I was Johnny on the spot. I knew the mentality of the club and the players, which Peter Withe didn't. I knew that Wimbledon was and still is a most unusual outfit ...'

Chapter Twenty-three

Sam Hammam has a slightly different version of the events which led up to Joe becoming manager of Wimbledon in January 1992. But then you might expect that. Sam after all had the overall view, even if he did not always understand the personal motives of all the participants.

'I don't know why Bobby Gould left. We are still good friends, we still speak, as I am with all my old managers. I can only think that Bobby left on an impulse. Bobby is one of the original hippies, a rolling stone, who likes to move on.

'I promoted Ray Harford as manager. That is my policy. To promote from within. When Ray left, to join Kenny Dalglish, I had every intention of making Joe the manager. That's why I'd made him assistant manager to Ray. When I make someone assistant manager, I am saying you are next in line.

'So when Ray left, I called Joe in. In my mind, I was expecting to make him manager, but what I said to him was, "Who do you think should be the next manager?" I honestly expected him to say, "You're looking at him, Sam." He didn't. He gave me names of likely people. It became clear to me that Joe was not convinced he could be the manager. He had talked himself out of it. That's how I felt at the time.

'I've told Joe this many times since, that he talked me out of it. I know he doesn't agree, that it didn't happen that way. But to me, that is the honest truth.

'I thought he could still make it, he had the qualities, but at that time, he didn't have the look of a manager. There was not enough about him. He needed more time, more confidence.

'So I began to think, perhaps Joe is right. After all, he had been out in the wilderness for what was it, 15 years since he'd left Spurs?'

Come on – managing Nepal and managing in Dubai is not exactly the wilderness. Sam made a face at this.

'You can be manager of China, as Ted Buxton was, with billions of people, but it means little over here. Those sort of overseas jobs come through the FA.'

Then what about his experience in England?

'What about it? Was he ever really appointed manager at Doncaster, or was he just caretaker manager? Anyway, that job didn't last long. His managerial experience was limited.

'But that wasn't my main worry. My worry was that Joe himself was worried. The players loved him. I loved him. But he just wasn't promoting himself as manager. That's why I decided to look elsewhere.

'I tried two people who wouldn't come and then I decided on Peter Withe. As always, I talk around. I ask about five or six people who have inside knowledge and will tell me the truth. If I get a bad report from someone, then I usually act upon it. I hear all their opinions, but I decide. My soundings on Peter Withe were good. Doug Ellis at Villa gave him a good report.

'But, very soon, oh in weeks, I realized it was a mistake. Peter was not the gung-ho type. He was too calm, too quiet, for Wimbledon. I had to correct it very quickly. So, yes, I did sack him, after only I think 104 days. And it was on the motorway, but not the same day as I appointed Joe.

'I was driving up the motorway to Scotland, to go goose shooting, yes goose, not grouse. I arranged to meet Peter in a motorway service station and I sacked him. It's the first time in all my years at Wimbledon I have sacked someone. All the others left, going on to better things. Or so they thought at the time. But I still love them all. They are still family.

'I then went on to Scotland for the few days' shooting. It was coming home down the motorway that I rang Joe and offered him the job. He had always been in my mind. That's how I like to do things, promoting the assistant.'

So that was good news for Joe, just when he feared he was going to be overlooked again. But how did Bonnie feel, with Joe about to take on, at the age of 45, the stresses and strains of his first 'proper' managerial job?

'I was pleased of course, when he got the coaching job at Wimbledon, after what had happened at Doncaster. The people up there were lovely, very friendly, but I felt like an alien. It filled me with horror to think that for the rest of my life, if Joe makes a go of this job, we could be here, in Doncaster, forever.

'When Joe got the sack at Doncaster, well when they gave his job to someone else, I have to admit I was quite happy. But poor old Joe. It took the stuffing out of him, what happened at Doncaster.

'So when Wimbledon came up, I was very pleased, whatever position he had, because at last he was with a London club.

'We did think of buying a house down there, near Plough Lane, or the training ground. We looked at a few and I was willing to move, though I have lived all my life in North London. Then we thought of what happened at Doncaster. In the end we moved to another house in North London, to this one here in Mill Hill. It gave me something to do, doing up the house, though I was still doing occasional part-time work at the dentist.

'It took Joe one and a half hours to get to work, so he had a tiring journey before he started. It was a learning curve, those first two years. Yes, he was devastated when he was overlooked. Twice it happened, really. He was going to give it only another year.

'I was delighted for Joe of course when Sam rang on his mobile from the motorway and offered him the manager's job, but at the same time my heart sank. I thought this is going to be a whole new chapter. What am I in for? Marriage to a player is one thing, but to a manager, that is something else. Will I ever see him again? I thought. Will he be totally stressed out, all consumed by his job from now on ...?'

Chapter Twenty-four

I got all the squad together for my first game in charge and told them straight. 'We're seriously in the shit. We'll have to win every game till the end of the season, or that's it. I want people playing for me with bottle, not anyone who shits themselves when the going gets tough.' I just spoke to them like that, as I normally would. I didn't change my approach from being trainer to manager. I was myself.

I brought back Corky and Sanchez, as I felt they were vital to the club spirit and could still do a job. No one thought I'd do it. The bookies were offering 9-4 that we would go down.

That first game was away to QPR, on 1 February 1992. Our team was Hans Segers in goal, then Cork, Phelan, Warren Barton, John Scales, Miller, Robbie Earle, John Fashanu, Laurie Sanchez, McAllister, Clarke. We made some crunching tackles, especially on Ray Wilkins, who was playing for QPR that day. He wasn't very pleased. We got a draw, 1-1. Fash scored from a penalty.

Next week, for my first game at home as manager, we beat Villa 2-0, with goals by Fash and Phelan. The crowd was small, just 5,500, but Sam made me go out and milk it, so I went and waved to our supporters.

We then had a good run – seven unbeaten games on the trot after I took over. We not only stayed up, which some people had doubted, but we ended up 13th, ahead of Chelsea and Spurs. That was the season Leeds won it. And West Ham went down. I got given a two-year contract as manager from Sam. I got more money, but not massive.

But I had no money to spend on players. I could also see that we were losing likely lads. We'd scout them, invite them to come to training, with their mums and dads – then they'd take one look at our scruffy premises and think what the hell ...

Terry Burton, who became my assistant manager, told me that he always tried if possible to sign kids in their own homes, not at our place. The kids, and their parents, had probably already been for trials at Arsenal, Chelsea, and Spurs, had lunch at their training ground, done the tour, seen all the wonderful facilities. Naturally they couldn't believe our place. They'd look around and say er, is that the first-team training over there? – and they'd be looking at the Dog and Duck.

Then of course the only place to eat was the greasy spoon transport caff. We all ate there all the time – very often before as well as after training. Yes, it's hard to believe, when you think of players' diets today and how careful they are. I'd do the same on arrival each morning, sit with them, chatting away. We'd have a sausage sandwich, a fried bacon sandwich, or whatever. I can see Corky now, stuffing his face. Ten years ago, that was normal, that was what English players did. Big fry-ups, with sauce poured all over it. Then they'd go out for training.

There was this bloke who served in the greasy spoon, Fag Ash Fred we called him. He had a fag in his mouth all the time, while he was making your bacon sandwich. He never took it out, so the ash got longer and longer. Eventually some ash would fall into the sandwich he was making, so the person next in the queue would say, 'Oh, I don't want that bacon sandwich Fred, I think I'll have the sausage instead.' Fred would stand behind the counter saying, 'So who's this bloody bacon sandwich for then?' Everyone would then move out of the way.

It was vital that we had better training premises as a top-division club. Not just for ourselves, but for attracting kids from home and abroad. I moaned about it to Sam. He knew all about it anyway and had tried to buy another place, but they were too expensive. So *what he did in the end was buy the transport caff. He knocked it through, redesigned it, put in a proper TV lounge. We took the car park as well, and got rid of the lorries.*

We decorated all the walls with photos of our stars and our big moments, like winning the Cup Final, or beating Manchester United. We'd have close-up pictures of our own stars, Vinnie Jones, Dennis Wise, Warren Barton, Alan Cork, Fash or Robbie Earle, faces most kids coming on trial would recognize. It let them see they could be a star, even at Wimbledon. At Spurs, we used to be surrounded by photos of the Double team. That could be a bit of a downer, thinking we'd never do as well, but it could also inspire you, show you the things that were possible.

We also got a proper dining room, kitchen and everything. Slowly the diets for all players began to change. I think it was the arrival of foreign players and foreign managers that helped the change. Not at Wimbledon. We never really had foreign players, but there were masses at all the other clubs, so it spread.

We were still at Plough Lane when I arrived, but then the Taylor Report came in and we failed it. We were told we had to shut it down. It was unsafe. We couldn't afford to develop it, so we looked around to share with another club, like Brentford or Fulham. But that didn't work.

Sam tried to get some millionaire to come into the club, help us build a new stadium, but nobody would. With us not being a glamorous team, they weren't interested. 'You won't be here long, will you,' they'd say, 'not in the Premier League. You'll be back down the divisions, probably back to the Southern League, so what's the point of investing money in Wimbledon.'

At Plough Lane, the manager's office was in a Portakabin. The stale smell of hot dogs wafted in from a stall just outside. Even in the dressing rooms, you could smell it.

The dressing rooms were awful anyway. I don't think they'd been changed since the non-league days. The away toilets had a bare light bulb on a flex hanging from the ceiling. On match days, we'd take the bulb out, making them have their shits in the dark. They'd come in, complaining, and I'd say oh sorry, we have a leak, some water's got in, we're waiting for the electricity people to repair it. It was just a trick. We did it every week, to wind up the other team, make them feel miserable. Today they call it 'warfare'. Wimbledon have been doing it for years.

But in the end we moved to Selhurst Park, sharing with Crystal Palace. I know our supporters hated it. We didn't like it either. Visiting teams and their supporters hated it as well. They'd say they couldn't find it. Travelling down there, through South London, is hell.

But Selhurst did give us a capacity of 27,000, whereas at Plough Lane I think the most we could get was 13,000 – but 5,000 was more like the average. At Selhurst, we had hospitality suites and private boxes, so the club began to have a lot more money coming in. So things began to get better all round, on and off the pitch.

Chapter Twenty-five

'What a transformation in a man,' says Sam Hammam. 'I knew he had it in him, but I was surprised how quickly he changed. You can only think someone can do a job. It's always a gamble. It's not till they actually do it, then you know. Two wins, and Joe was so self-assured, so confident.

'This happens all the time in football. With a manager and with the team. Two wins, and they are strutting around. Two defeats, and you think they've lost it forever.

'The players loved Joe anyway. I always knew that, but now they loved him even more. He's a very funny man, and so amiable.'

Did the players get him the job, which is what Joe himself thinks?

'No, Joe got himself the job – through his own qualities. He did do a great job that season when he took over. We were 17th, but I think we had two or three games in hand, so it wasn't as serious a situation as it looked. But something had to be done – and Joe did it. Within two weeks, I thought he's my man. I will support Joe 100 per cent forever – and I have done, ever since.

'Joe can come over bombastic and aggressive, but I think he is a shy man, and very very loving. With the players, out on the training ground or beside the pitch, that is your man. You see then that he is a genius. Away from football, he's quiet.

'It's the same with rock stars. I have got to know quite a few of them. On the stage, they are brilliant. Off stage they can be socially shy.

'Yes. I did use the word "genius". I think Joe does have it as a football manager. I don't think he could do anything else nearly as well.'

So what has he got?

'Well technically he certainly has it. I could see that right away. I might not be a football expert, but over the years I have observed at very close quarters what happens. I have always gone in the dressing room, watched them training, been there all the time. I don't interfere. I just observe.

'Now, we knew that Joe was a good coach. We had seen that under Ray. Being a manager is different. Until you actually pick the team, set the tactics, then make changes when things go wrong, you don't know if someone will make a good manager.

'I would be there at team meetings, hear what his tactics were going to be, and why – then I'd watch it happening. I loved observing Joe. It was a miracle sometimes, magical, watching it all unfold. That's what I've grown to love about football. Not just winning or playing well, but following all the strategies.

'I've watched Joe reacting to events, making changes when the other team had spotted our strengths, or when they made changes to make the most of our weaknesses. Joe is excellent at this.'

Was he your best ever manager? Sam naturally would not rise to this, unwilling to make comparisons. On several occasions he had said how Dave Bassett was his type, and of course it was Dave who got them through the divisions. Then Bobby Gould had actually won something, the FA Cup. On the other hand, it was Joe who kept them there, in the Premiership, despite all the odds, all the doubters.

Though Sam refused to put his managers in order, he was more than willing to give his list of what he considered the qualities needed in a Wimbledon manager. Eight qualities, he said, which he went on to enumerate. Sam, over the years, has acquired some crude cockney phrases, picked up from some crude cockney footballers, which are amusing when mixed up with his sudden flashes of Arab invective, but at heart he is a very logical thinker with a cultivated mind and a sharp brain.

'One, I put loyalty. To Wimbledon, the team, to me. I don't want a manager who is thinking from the beginning that he will move on, that if Charlton, say, offers more money, which they well might, that he'll take it and leave. There is no point in looking for the so-called "best" man available. If I suspect he won't have loyalty, then he won't stay and I don't want him.

'Two, honesty. I don't want anyone who is corrupt financially or morally.

'Three, hard work. Top people may often not appear to work hard, but they do. Pete Sampras can practise the same shot for five hours, to make it look effortless, but the public don't know that. They don't see the hundreds of painful, tedious, boring hours which have to be put in if you want to be a champion. Joe might appear jovial, one of the lads, but he is certainly a hard worker. He put in the hours. No more hours than me. I have done more hours for Wimbledon than any manager has done. But Joe did work very hard.

'Four, technical ability. By this I mean the ability to get the best possible out of the team, out of what he has. You might be able to drive the same car as Schumacher, but you are not going to get out of it what he can get. A good manager has to spot the weakness of the other team, expose it, and plug the gaps in our weakness. He must have a game-plan, then he must execute it. That is what I mean by technical. Watching Joe, I always knew I was watching a master at work.

'Five, ability to spot talent – to find or buy players, then develop them into better players.

'Six, motivation. He must be able to make them do better than they are doing, pull them up when they are down.

'Seven, ability to handle the media.

'Eight, organizational skills.'

Without comparing Joe with your other managers, how does he rate under those eight headings?

'If you find a manager who is outstanding in three or four of those eight categories, then you are doing well. No one is ever outstanding in all eight. No one. I would say Joe is outstanding in six of them, the first six, so that is very high. On the last two, I would say, let me think, Joe is very good.

'With the media, the press loved him. He gave them good quotes. He amused them and he amused me. I love him, as you know. With the media, and with his organization, he had his own way of doing things. Let us say it was not exactly a straight river. My mind flows logically. Joe's mind is perhaps like your mind, a river which meanders, which fills up, which empties. But it is a very good mind, all the same.'

Chapter Twenty-six

John Fashanu was captain when I arrived. Fash was God. Huge character and so vital to the team. No problems to look after. Easy as pie.

About my first purchase was Vinnie Jones from Chelsea in September 1992. He had been at Wimbledon for two years before, 1986-88, when they'd won the FA Cup. He immediately said he wanted to be captain.

Me and Sam had had long discussions about bringing Vinnie back. He thought it might be a risk, bringing someone back to his old club. He might think he's outgrown it, and won't try as hard. I didn't have any worries. He was a great buy for us, a real leader.

I'd never come across Vinnie in my professional career, but I had known of him practically all his life. He's also from Watford. I knew his family, his brothers. My sister Shirley is a friend of his family. His early career was the same as mine – Watford Boys, Hertfordshire Boys. I paid £750,000 for him with no worries. And I made him club captain. Fash then became team captain. Fash didn't complain. He was still captain out on the pitch.

Having Fash and Vinnie made us so strong, so feared. Teams were scared to play us. I made the most of it, of course. Talking to the press, I'd say no team wanted to play us. And in the dressing room I'd say the same, telling my players the other team have just arrived and some of them look terrified, so get stuck in, make them aware of it, give them reason to be scared.

Fash was brilliant. After some clash he'd say, ever so gently and nicely, 'What, me? I never touched him. Is he really on the treatment table? I just never realized.'

Fash had blistering pace, phenomenal heading ability, huge balls. He wasn't scared of any centre half, however massive. He always gave as good as he got. It can happen that your striker gets dominated by a centre half, disappears in a match. Fash did have the odd off day, but even then, he would still contribute. His only weak point was his finishing. That could have been better. But he did his bit for the Crazies.

During the 1994 World Cup finals in the USA, Fash was out there as a TV commentator. Nigeria was playing, so he did all their matches. Ron Atkinson was with him as well, up in the gantry. They must have got talking, that's my theory, because very late one evening, when I was at home, I got this call from Fash. 'Hello, gaffer. Fash here – would you let me go to Villa? My career is coming to an end, I've given Wimbledon 10 years' loyal service, so will you let me go?'

He was 32 at the time. We'd never thought of selling him, though we knew he would soon have to be replaced.

'Well if you were selling me,' he said, 'how much?'

I said I didn't know. He said go on, just give me a figure. So I said a million at least. But it would be up to Sam. Sam does all transfers and money. I'd have to talk to him. So I rang Sam and said I think I could get a million for Fash. And I think the timing is right, for him and for us. I did have Dean Holdsworth as a striker and Marcus Gayle. He'd been a left winger for Brentford but I turned him into a striker. I then bought Efan Ekoku from Norwich for £750,000. I thought he might be hungrier. So I felt we could manage without Fash, though he was a loss.

Fash had only a dozen games for Villa – then his cruciate ligaments went, and that was it. Such bad luck – career over. He was okay financially. He had insured himself well, and so had the club, so he did all right. And of course he was wealthy in his own right, with all his TV work and property.

When I became manager, I started watching first teams for a change. As reserves manager, I'd just watched other reserves, or lower league teams. Now I did both. Watched the opposition, look-

ing for weaknesses, and also did the lower teams, looking for players. So it increased my time on the road. Terry would do likewise.

But the big problem all the time was money. We had to buy cheap, but we also had to try to keep the players we had discovered, the ones we'd made good. I had this continual worry that someone was after one of my players. I was never worried about my situation. I always felt my job was secure. But every day when I went in for training I knew there would be some press story, some rumour, about one of my players being tapped.

Direct approaches are illegal. A manager can't contact your players direct. They have to talk to his manager. But of course they do, or get intermediaries to do it. Their agents do it, agree a plot between themselves, then give out a story to the press, which isn't true, hasn't happened, but just unsettles everyone.

Our strength at Wimbledon was our fantastic club harmony, but these rumours can muck up any team spirit. You have to be strong and tough not to be unsettled by stories of some big glamour club being after you.

We knew that Liverpool was interested in John Scales, because we'd read about it. He'd read about it, even though we knew nothing, and nothing had happened. Same with Warren Barton and Newcastle. The better my team did, the more prominence they got in the newspapers and TV – and the more I knew the chances were I'd lose them.

I've never rung a player in my life. I can honestly say that. When I went to watch Brentford, say, I'd talk to the manager afterwards. If it was someone like Steve Perryman, who was a friend I'd played with, I'd say, 'How much do you want for so and so?' He'd say we're not selling. I'd say yeah, but how much. Then I'd make an offer. Then another offer, one they couldn't refuse. I got Marcus Gayle for only £250,000 from Brentford. That was a brilliant deal for me, but not so much for Steve. I was the winner on that one, but he needed the money at the time.

When I first became the manager, I did think back a lot to my time under Bill Nicholson, how he did things. I have nothing but admiration for him, but he'd say you have to watch George Best, he'll kill

148

you, and don't let Denis Law turn or you've had it, till you began to think, fucking hell it's hardly worth going out there. He thought if you were picked for the next match, that was enough praise. He didn't have to say anything else. He didn't go in for any of that arm-round-you stuff.

So I thought of what he'd done and hadn't done, then I thought I'll just be myself, to talk and act as I'd always done.

I do tend to say things that come into my head, have a laugh and a joke with everyone. So from the beginning I didn't hold back when talking to the press, treating them like I would anyone else. After Peter Withe had gone, and everyone by then knew about his keen-ness for insisting on blazers and stuff, I was asked what my clothes policy would be. I said I didn't care what my players wore. They could wear knickers and suspenders if they liked – but not till after training. That wasn't prepared, just a joke that came out.

Sometimes I did get into trouble, for shooting my mouth off before thinking. I'd lash out at the referees, if I thought they'd got a decision wrong. I called Mike Reed a Little Hitler and said that Paul Alcock was All Cock and No Balls. It was out of order and I got rightly hauled up before the FA about the Mike Reed remark.

I also got done for swearing at Newcastle. I turned to some people in the crowd behind me, who'd been winding me up, and said 'Go fuck off'. Their police chief got me for that – saying they had orders to evict anyone from the ground for using obscene or abusive language. At my FA hearing, I played the video tape from the match, turned up the volume high, and you could clearly hear 30,000 Geordies chanting 'Who's the wanker in the black'. So I says, did the police evict all 30,000 of them? Course not. Anyway, I got fined £20,000, or something like that, and banned from the touch-line for four weeks. Another time I got fined £10,000.

I do feel sorry for refs, which is why I think there should be a fourth set of eyes – another official sitting watching it on TV, with instant replays of anything dodgy in the penalty box, or when a ball hits the woodwork and goes half over the line. The ref would be told on his earphone if it was a penalty or goal or not. The crowd would be instantly told the decision as well, and they couldn't blame the

Team talk

Hallelujah!

I sn't it wonderful to welcome Alex Ferguson and his Manchester United players to Selhurst Park this afternoon in what should be a marvellous atmosphere.

We all witnessed the emotional scenes at Old Trafford on Monday night when Steve Bruce and Bryan Robson went up to collect the Premier League trophy.

It was an occasion I'm sure you'd all agree was very moving and our congratulations go to the club for their achievement.

Even up until two weeks ago the general opinion was that United would be coming here for their last game needing a result to clinch the Premier League title.

The fact that so many experts in the game believed we were capable of robbing them of that honour is a great compliment to all of us at the club.

While we sincerely congratulate United, we're determined to have our own party this afternoon and end the season on a winning note.

If nothing else our fantastic fans who stuck by us during those dark winter months deserve it. We want to show you how much

we've appreciated your magnificent support through the hard times and finish what turned out to be a great season in style.

It was you the fans that stayed loyal during a season that for long spells robbed us of some of our most experienced players through injury, and encouraged the youngsters that filled the gaps.

During the course of the campaign those same youngsters like Neal Ardley and Gerald Dobbs have emerged as true Wimbledon men.

I would also like to take this opportunity to thank everyone who has worked tirelessly behind the scenes from Sam, Ned, chairman Stanley Reed, Dave and the rest of the

board at the very top to my right hand man Terry Burton. I'd also like to thank all of my coaching staff including chief scout Ron Suart, my lush physio Steve Allen, Pinky and Perky (alias kit men Sid and Joe) and last but by no means least, all you wonderful fans.

Have a great day and give the lads one final last big cheer this afternoon. My thanks to everybody.

Cheers.

Joe Kinnear

Flashback – Joe seen here against Manchester United's 1967 championship team. Also in the picture are George Best and Denis Law.

THIS PAGE SPONSORED BY JAN AND SARAH

5

Wimbledon programme, v. Manchester United, May 9, 1993

On the touchline in his first full season as Wimbledon manager. ©Action Images

Signing Dean Holdsworth. ©Anton Want/Allsport

A day out go-kart racing. Ninety-year-old Stanley Reed was the star of the show. That's me wearing Stanley's glasses.

On the bench with assistant Terry Burton. ©Action Images

With Sam Hammam after holding Manchester United to a 1-1 draw at Old Trafford in the FA Cup 4th round in January 1997. ©Action Images

Vinnie Jones, who Joe
made captain after his
return to Wimbledon as
Joe's first signing.
©Michael Steele/Empics

Joe receiving one of his
many Carling Manager
of the Month awards.
©Action Images

Above: Joe has a word with Robbie Earle in the ho[...] game against Sheffield Wednesday in September 19[...] ©Action Images

Left: Marcus Gayle, at the start of the 1998/9 seaso[...] ©Tom Honan/ Empics

Below: Joe is joined on the touchline by Sam Ham[...] ©John Marsh/ Empics

Crazy gang inauguration for John Hartson, Joe's record signing at Wimbledon. His clothes are set on fire… and then he's gently guided towards a large puddle. ©Action Images

Joe receiving his Sky Sports Manager of the Year award, voted for by the viewers, in 1996.

Joe at fifty, training with the Crazy Gang squad.

Joe meeting Mary Robinson, then President of Eire.

With Vinnie and Sam at the races at Sandown.

Joe and Bonnie at their daughter Russelle's wedding in 1996.

Presenting his friend Alex Ferguson with the Manager of the Year award, at the League Managers' Association dinner in May 1999. He was actually returning the favour as Alex had handed Joe the same award in 1994.

ref. It could be on a big screen, so they would all cheer or all boo.

Anyway, in my first full season in charge, 1992-93, we finished 12th, so we'd gone up one place from the previous season. In the next season we did really well and got to 6th. The season after that we were 9th. I was winning awards by then, Manager of the Month and that, Managers' Manager of the Year, so I must have been doing something right. People were not predicting at the beginning of every season we would go down. We had stabilized as a club in the top half of the division. Not bad was it, for the Crazy Gang.

Chapter Twenty-seven

Sam has said he is not crazy, but it was a pretty crazy thing to do, buying Wimbledon, a pig in a poke, a shot in the dark, then becoming so besotted by it that for over 20 years he lived and breathed the club, looking up it as part of his family.

He insists, for example, that every new member of staff signs a contract forbidding them from divulging, now and forever, secrets about the club. This is why not a great deal of first person stuff, from the inside, has made its way into books or newspapers. It was noticeable that in Vinnie Jones's biography he had very little to say about his Wimbledon years.

There were of course rumours, apocryphal stories about their initiation ceremonies, but I never knew how true they were.

'Oh, mostly true,' said Sam. 'At Wimbledon we have always done crazy things when new players arrive. Naturally they come in their best clothes, for their first day, strip off in the dressing room, then go to the lavatory or out to training. When they come back, they find their clothes have been burned. Put in a pile, in the middle of the dressing room, and set alight. I have done it myself. I like people who do crazy things, childish, innocent things. And sometimes I do them myself.

'Being a new club in the league, we didn't have the fine old traditions of Arsenal or Spurs, things going back so many years, or teams and stars everyone knows about. Nobody knew us. We had no history. We were outsiders, a small club, with small crowds. So I traded on these crazy things. Some were just artificial, done for effect, to make us look crazy, but we did do them.

'For example, since I came to Wimbledon, and began running the club full time, I have had it written into the contract of every new player and manager that if we ever lose by four goals, they will have to go, in full evening dress, to a ballet of my choice. I can show you the contracts. I don't always exercise the right, but I have done, on occasions. I made Vinnie Jones do it once. He met a very nice ballerina there, so he was quite grateful ...

'The next punishment is to go twice a year to a Lebanese restaurant of my choice. And there they have to eat sheep's bollocks, stuffed intestines and camel's brains. Oh I've made them do it. Over the years I've picked on some to be punished. So far they haven't had to eat camel. There's never been camel available so far in London's Lebanese restaurants. But you can get sheep's bollocks, and I've made them eat it. It amused me to do it, even though it is childish. But it was part of the Crazy Gang image, to help give us a character.

'One of the things I like about Joe is that he has a crazy streak. He is serious about his work, but he can be playful. I am the same. I like to think I am still youthful. I like to think I'll be forever young. Even at 80, I hope I won't be colourless.

'By playful, I don't mean he is nasty. Just childlike. I remember in Tenerife once, with the team. We were staying in this big hotel with an atrium. Joe's bedroom was on the fourth floor. In the middle of the night, about five in the morning, he came out of his room and threw down a massive plant. It was huge, you could hardly lift it. It fell all the way down the four floors, into the bottom of the atrium ...'

That doesn't sound playful. That sounds drunk.

'Oh not at five in the morning. There had been a loud party and Joe couldn't get to sleep. Lucky it was five in the morning, or someone might have got hurt. I had to clear up the mess, sort it out with the management. I've had to do that several times over the years.'

For what sort of incidents? Do tell.

'No, that's enough. Some stories I can't repeat. But I always find Joe funny. The things he says make me laugh. I would never say them, never even think of saying them.

'One thing I've heard him say to total strangers who were knocking the Crazy Cang is "So you've survived the plane crash then?"

'They are always so taken aback. "Did you come down on a parachute then," Joe will continue. He's just trying to provoke them. I don't know why. That's Joe. It's his sense of humour, winding people up. He gives it and he can take it.

'Another time there was this huge girl who came up to us in a bar, also in Norway. Massive girl, very tall, very fat, dressed all in white. When she hears we are from London, she starts chatting to us, saying she would like to work in London. So Joe says, come and work for us. She asks what Joe does and he says he's a football manager. "What can I do for you?" she asks.

' "Well," says Joe, "in the summer, we play cricket and you would make a brilliant sight screen." She takes all this in, but doesn't quite understand. So she asks what she'll do in the football season.

' "Oh we'll use you in training," says Joe. "You'll just stand there and we'll run round..." Yes, a bit rude, as she was very fat. But I thought it was funny.

'Some times it can lead to trouble. We were once in a bar, all the team, plus one stranger who happened to be sitting at the bar when we arrived. He didn't move, when we all came in but he started to take the piss out of the Crazy Gang, so Joe says to him to his face, "Stop taking the piss."

'The guy ignored him at first, so Joe says it again. The guy then says he's a black belt at judo, so Joe better not say that again. Joe does, so the guy starts taking off his jacket, then does a few judo moves, punching and kicking the air, just to let us see he's serious. Joe is still laughing at him, he seems nuts. It's just about to get serious, when Fash pulls them apart. Fash saved the day.

'I didn't mind what Joe did. It amused me. I think in a high-pressure life, you need some joyful distractions. Pop musicians relax from their high pressures with drugs or women. Footballers relax by being playful. That's all it is. It's their idea of fun. It's childish, but they are all young people.

'We all wish that God will give us good health and happiness, but we also want God to give us youth and youthfulness. Some silly things you can't do with age. Streaking at Twickenham when you are 25 is one thing, but not at my age. I might think about it, but it wouldn't be proper.

'I myself hardly drink or smoke and I don't womanize, but I don't object to others being playful, as long as they don't overstep the mark. There is a certain line.

'That's why I have always insisted in every contract that no one, no player, no manager, can write or talk about Wimbledon without my permission. A manager after a game can talk about the game, but he can't talk about the club, about what we do behind the scenes. There are some things we don't want reported. I don't want anything which reflects badly on the club that I love.'

There was one reported incident about Sam himself, when he appeared to be a bit too playful, allegedly spraying graffiti over the dressing room wall when they were playing at West Ham. Was it true?

'It was exaggerated. I didn't write anything on the actual walls, just on a noticeboard, the tactics board. You do it with a felt pen, then it gets wiped out later.'

And what did you write?

'I just wanted to gee my players up, wind them up, so I wrote silly things.'

Such as?

' "Vinnie is shit", that sort of thing. Nothing serious ...'

When reporters do upset Sam, by writing things about the club he does not approve of, or are not true, then Sam has his own form of revenge. He calls them baptismals.

'I don't mind fair comment. If a reporter writes that the team plays rubbish, or a player is useless, that's their opinion. It's when they pick on a player's personal life, follow him to see if he is having an affair, that's what I object to. They do stalk certain players to get stories.

'I have two reporters on my list at present I'm waiting to get. And a third I'm thinking about.'

What will happen to them, if they are on your little list?

'The next time they come to report on one of our matches, or come to our training ground, they will be captured. Firstly they will have water buckets emptied over their heads. Next a bucket of blackcurrant juice. For a serious offence, they will be stripped naked and dragged across the grass then thrown in the water.'

How often has this happened?

'It is partly a warning, letting the offending person know what might happen to them. If they throw shit at us, we will throw shit back at them. It has happened at least once. No, I'm not naming names. They know who they are. It's up to them to admit we baptised them.'

Chapter Twenty-eight

At a club like Wimbledon, we were permanently concerned with balancing the books and never getting into debt. Sam was always saying, 'I won't go to bed with a sword over my head.' He boasted we were the only club in the Premier League never to get into debt. So if I had someone in mind to buy, I had to think of selling first. Or if someone came in to buy, I was immediately thinking of who I might be able to get with the money.

Warren Barton was bought for £250,000 in 1990. I watched him playing three times for Maidstone United, just after I'd joined the club. We then sold him in 1995 to Newcastle for £5 million. With that £5 million, I was able to buy three players. One of them was Duncan Jupp. I got him for £200,000 from Fulham. That was the sort of price I tried to buy players for. I got Kenny Cunningham for half a million from Millwall. He must be worth £7 million by now. Ben Thatcher cost us £1.9 million, the most at the time we had ever paid. He should be in the England team by now. He's the best uncapped left back in the Premiership. Better in the air than Le Saux. In 1998 we then paid £2 million each for Mark Kennedy and Andy Roberts.

Oyvind Leonhardsen was the only foreign player I bought. I got him from Rosenborg in 1994. He was playing for Norway, doing well, but everyone had had a look at him and didn't fancy him. They much preferred Flo and Solskjaer. I hadn't a chance of tempting them as they were getting fixed up with bigger clubs – Chelsea and Manchester United. They didn't fancy Leo as he was too small, *wasn't the best tackler and not so great at heading. But I could see what he did have – ball skill and hard work. He cost just half a million, spread over some time.*

'He's only five-feet nothing. When he turned up at training first day, Vinnie saw him and couldn't believe it. He went into the dressing room ahead of him. "The gaffer's only gone off his head," he told everyone. "Now he's gone and bought Jimmy Clitheroe."'

He was a very serious person when he arrived. The only one in the whole squad who didn't drink. It was a bit hard for him to understand the Crazy Gang mentality, but he was desperate to do well and to socialize with them. He would drink a glass of water while they were on pints of lager.

He was a bit nervous in training at first, but as fit as a flea. He'd run like a maniac, as much at the beginning of a game as at the end. He prefers a central midfield role, but I had Vinnie and Robbie there, so he had to play a bit wider, but he did it, and did it well.

I don't know why he decided to leave in 1997. It was nothing to do with us. I think it was because he was close to the Norwegian in the Liverpool team, Bjornebye, who'd also come from Rosenborg. Probably with speaking to him, hearing all about Liverpool, it made him dissatisfied. He said he wanted to go to a club which would win trophies. So I said "Why Liverpool then?' Sorry, it's my sense of humour. So we let him go. We sold him for £3.5 million – so it was good business. But the interesting thing was that Liverpool were the only Premiership club that came in for him.

Then of course he didn't settle up there. I don't know why. I can only think it was lack of confidence, not being given a decent run in the team. He shone with us, but then we did try hard to keep his pecker up. If he looked like getting depressed, and going into his shell, which he could do, then we worked on him. I hope he does well at Spurs, they seem to like him. I like to think my judgement was spot on. He is a first-class player.

The most money we ever paid was of course for John Hartson: £7 million from West Ham in January 1999. That surprised everyone. It was quite unexpected, really, not properly planned in advance. At the time, we happened to have some money in the kitty.

I'd heard about Hartson's fight in training at West Ham with Berkovic and it seemed as if he was on the way out. I'd only got that story from the papers, so I didn't know if it was true. I rang Harry Redknapp. 'What's the score, Harry, is he going?' 'For the right money, he might be,' said Harry. I was just trying it on, not expecting anything, except get lost. 'It's up to you,' said Harry. 'Make us a bid, but he won't be cheap.'

I talked to Sam about him. Hartson was only 23, so he had a lot of mileage in him. George Graham, while at Arsenal, had paid £2 million for him from Luton while he was still a teenager. We had some haggling with Harry and we stuck for a while at £6 million.

My thinking was long term. At 26-27, if he improves, he'll be coming to his peak, by which time Alan Shearer and Dion Dublin will have gone. Who else will there be who is a potent centre forward, of his age? Yes, Emile Heskey is one. I've tried and failed to buy him. He and Hartson are both players with potential.

Robbie Keane went for the same sort of money, around the same time. I knew about him. I keep in touch with all the Irish lads, but I don't think I would have got him. Anyway, it was taking more of a chance with him, coming from Wolves, with no Premier League experience. Hartson seemed to me a solid bet.

At Wimbledon, we're always going to find it hard to tempt the big foreign stars. We're never going to get the Bergkamps, Zolas and the Kanus. We have to be realistic, work out who we might get and who might agree to come. Hartson fitted the bill. He would do us for several years to come, with a bit of luck. He'd score the goals we needed.

With Leo gone to Liverpool and Deano gone to Bolton we had lost their 25 goals per season. But we had received a total of £7 million for them. So we agreed on £7 million for Hartson. We paid half up front and the rest a bit later. Sam also of course had a big wage bill to pay. I think he came on £10,000 a week wages.

The football world was amazed – that Wimbledon of all clubs had managed to find all that money. I bought him injured, which was bad luck. We played him when he was still not quite ready, patching him up, even though he had missed proper training. His first game for us was away to Spurs and he was up against Sol Campbell. I put him up front, on his own, so that was a right battle. We got a draw, 0-0.

But he wasn't properly fit. He missed more games and didn't show his best. People were still against him, for hitting Berkovic. By the end of the season, everyone was saying he was the worst buy of the season, that I'd made a big mistake.

I'm not against the press writing nasty things. They are all entitled to their views. Bad things written in the press can jog you, make you think, hmm, they might have a point. Very often the headline is the worst, more sensational than the story itself.

But I still had faith in him. I knew he was carrying an injury when I'd had to play him. Then when he was out, he put on weight. I knew we weren't getting the real John Hartson.

I signed him on a seven-year contract. About the longest we'd ever given anyone. I still think he's a good buy. One for the future. Signing him for seven years meant the club is in control of the lad.

I know for a fact that £5 million has been offered for him – plus a couple of other players in exchange. Proves my judgement was right, if others value him that highly.

But whether we make a profit in the end or not, doesn't really matter. Hartson is the sort of player who will give you 15 goals every season, the way Fash did, or Dean Holdsworth, Efan Ekoku. All clubs want that sort of consistent striker. I know that Harts is a 20-goal-a-season player when he's super fit and injury-free. Time will tell.

Chapter Twenty-nine

Buying players is always a matter of luck – whether they'll settle in, settle down, improve and do well for you. Managing players is much harder and you need experience in knowing how to handle them.

I looked upon Vinnie Jones and Robbie Earle as almost part of my coaching team. They were such strong characters, on and off the pitch. They would come to me and tell me things, or tell me off. I sometimes was too hard on players, especially those who had grown up in the club, started with us as kids. I suppose I looked upon them as part of the family. You can give them a bollocking, the way you would with your own kids, thinking they can take it, they'll understand. With players I'd bought, I probably held back a bit more.

If I ever did go a bit over the top, screaming and shouting at someone, Vinnie or Robbie would come in and say, Gaffer, I think you went a bit far with Marcus Gayle or Neil Ardley or whoever it might have been. Perhaps an arm round their shoulder might cheer them up. I'd take their advice. You don't want players going around all sulky. Some do need arms. Others need a kick up the arse.

I always try to say what I have to say straight afterwards in the dressing room, not bottle it up for later. Sometimes we'd be in the dressing room till 6.30, if I was having a right go at them. I remember one evening game at Charlton. It was midnight, and I was still rabbiting on. All the Charlton people had gone home. The other rooms were locked. The caretaker comes in wanting to put the lights out.

It's more a clearing of the air, not bollocking them. I did let them have their say, encouraged them to say what they thought had gone wrong. I didn't mind them answering back. I liked that. After that Charlton game, I at least left feeling positive, that we'd talked things out. I don't know what they thought, but it made me feel happier.

I always try to smell out people harbouring bad thoughts. You can't keep them all happy all the time. Whenever you pick the team, someone is hurt and upset. You just have to be honest with them.

I always tried to take the long view. Few players hit instant form. You have to look ahead, over a whole season, not just two poor games. When players lose form, you have to be patient. The player himself is often not aware of a loss of form but the players around him can see it. He thinks he's trying as hard, training as well, doing everything just the same. Very often he might score a brilliant goal, and for a moment all his sins are forgotten, at least with the fans. But you know his poor form is still there. You've seen it. On the video, you can point out the chances he didn't take, the headers he missed.

On Mondays, after some light training, I'd show a video of the weekend match. I'd have watched it several times myself, made notes, bits I wanted to focus on. We called it the Horror Show. I would show incidents where we were caught out of position. I'd freeze the film, ask each person what they thought they were doing. We'd go over what could have been done, how a shout should have been given, or just more concentration.

Many players of course don't take it in. They're not interested. All they want to know is if they are in the team, have they got a shirt. They don't even care where they play.

But every game throws up a problem, shows a weakness you've not been aware of, either about ourselves or the opposition.

We know other teams are watching us as well, just as carefully, which is why you vary your normal set pieces, every so often. I always changed at least one thing for every match, threw in one different set piece. That's why it's vital to know the line-up of the other team as soon as possible, so you can work out what tactics they might have been working on. I noticed when Chelsea played us they usually played big – putting on bigger players, more six-footers than normal.

I always made a point of never ever talking about tiredness when something had gone wrong. I would never say, 'You was leggy there.' I didn't want to put that idea into their head. Being tired is just an excuse. I know, and they know, how hard they have trained. I know they're fucking fit because I've run them into the ground. Even if I've read in the papers that some of them have been out shagging all night, or clubbing, I'd never refer to that. Mention tiredness, for whatever reason, and it seeps into their heads.

When that happens, the next stage is not feeling so good, feeling aches and pains. There are clubs where there's always a gang of players in the treatment room. I don't allow that.

Vinnie Jones was the sort who hated to be injured, who would deny it, wanting to play on. There was one game, fairly early on, when we'd had a good result against Liverpool on the Saturday, but Vinnie had taken a knock. I could tell in training on Monday he wasn't right. We had an evening match against Arsenal on the Tuesday evening, at Highbury, so I decided not to play him.

He came to my house in the afternoon, as he lives not far away. We'd arranged to drive there together. We sat in the garden and I told him I wasn't playing him as he wasn't 100 per cent. He was furious of course. Bonnie comes out into the garden and says, 'Like a drink Vinnie, cup of tea?' He says, 'I'll have a beer, darling, as I'm not sodding playing.' So Bonnie brings him a Budweiser.

At Highbury, some time before kick-off, I tell him to go out and warm up. I haven't announced he's not playing, just to confuse Arsenal. He's warming up on the pitch, talking to Ian Wright, when they both look up into the stand and Wrighty says, 'Isn't that Mike Smith?' Now Mike Smith had just been appointed manager of Wales. 'He's come to see you, Vinnie,' says Wrighty.

Vinnie comes rushing over to me, pleading with me to play him, this is his big chance, Mike Smith has come all the way from Wales to see him specially. I tell Vinnie to do some fast jogging, see how he feels. Vinnie belts up and down and says he's as fit as a flea, raring to go. So 'gainst my better judgement, I decided to play him.

Guess what happens? He only has a blinder. We beat Arsenal 1-0. Vinnie gets the winning goal – and gets his first cap for Wales. The moral is clear: have a Budweiser before every game ...

The image of Wimbledon was that we would run any team off the park. We would never let them settle for a second. I needed Wimbledon to believe this, as well as the opposition. So any talk of tiredness was out.

And it was true. We collectively hassled all over the pitch. We knew of course that if we stood back and let them play, let them come at us, they'd beat us. Because they were likely to have the better individual players.

After a few years, as we progressed, I was able to find players with more vision. When that happened, you did get a different sort of player wanting to join us. But basically our strength was in our tactics and in our set plays.

It was hard graft, keeping up the standards, keeping Wimbledon up the league, but the more I succeeded, the more I was remunerated. I think I was on £50,000 a year when I was first appointed manager, but had bonuses as well, depending on our league position, Cup runs and things. So I suppose that brought me up to £100,000 a year.

The senior players, in 1990 when I arrived, were getting much the same – around a basic £1,000 a week – or £50,000. That's what people like Alan Cork and Laurie Sanchez were getting. They'd been there for years but were getting towards the end of their careers. It seemed a lot to them at the time – but I should think they can't believe it now. In just 10 years, many Premier League players, even a couple at Wimbledon, are getting 10 times that.

The top wage at Wimbledon when I left was about £10,000 a week. Most were probably on between £5,000 and £8,000, as their basic wage. Then there can be very good bonuses for points and goals. Sam had Fash on £10,000 a goal on his last contract – but his basic wage was only £90 per week. Knock in three goals in a game, and he could have himself an extra £30,000.

Wimbledon might not have the gates, or the sponsorship money, but if you stay in the Premier League, you have the TV income. At the end, counting all my bonuses and things, I was getting £500,000 a year. Average, I suppose for the Premier League. I assume Fergie, Vialli, George Graham and Wenger are getting about a million a year. I'm told when Martin O'Neill was at Leicester he was getting £750,000 a year, but I can't quite believe it. I wouldn't expect Bradford or Watford to be able to pay that sort of money, or Southampton or Sheffield Wednesday. Sam used to tell me I was in the top six best-paid managers. I expect it was more like the top 12, but even so, I was very grateful and very happy. And he did always tell me I had a job for life at Wimbledon.

Other clubs were said to have come in for me, though I was never approached personally. Just what I read in the papers. Sam didn't tell me if there were any approaches, obviously, as he didn't want me to get itchy feet. But Celtic is supposed to have been interested in me. Everton at one time, even Liverpool.

Then there was Spurs. I was always being tipped for that, whenever anyone left. Around the time Christian Gross was getting the push, I was approached by a consortium involving Richard Littlejohn, the journalist and broadcaster, and Paul Miller. He used to play for Spurs and is now a financial man. I don't know who was in their consortium, where the money was coming from. They just approached me, saying they were planning a takeover deal because Alan Sugar had said he was fed up and was thinking of selling his Spurs shares. So they'd got together an offer. I was told that if it was accepted, they wanted me to become Spurs manager. I said I'd be interested. It wasn't my doing, I wasn't in their consortium. They just came to me.

Anyway, Sugar in the end told them to piss off. And he was furious with me, apparently. I told him the offer had nothing to do with me. Of course I would have loved to have gone to Spurs, gone back to my old club as manager. I still do. Why not?

But I was loving Wimbledon, everything about it. I was always happy there. It suited me, the Wimbledon attitude, the Crazy Gang mentality. That was me, really. I gave it my heart and soul.

I enjoyed all the tricks they played, the initiation ceremonies.

Some would be minor, like having the sleeves cut off their jackets during their first day at training. Or they might be stripped naked and taken out and thrown in a pond of water. That could be nasty in winter-time.

There was one player I bought at the end of the season, so he missed that season's training sessions. But of course the players hadn't forgotten. In the close season, we went off to Spain for a few days and were in this big posh hotel. I was sitting with our chairman, Stanley Reed, in the lobby of the hotel, having a chat and a glass of wine. All the players were sitting around the corner, in this big reception area, with lots of plants and trees and a glass lift which was going up and down. I could hear them laughing, and just thought it's the usual jokes and wind-ups.

The hotel manager comes over to me and says could he have a word. I says what's the problem? He says please follow me. We go over to the big reception area where this glass lift is going up and down. The players are all pointing up at it, laughing and shouting, so are some of the hotel guests. But I couldn't see what they were on about until the lift came down. A group of guests stepped forward to go in – and there was my new summer signing. He was inside, tied up and half-naked, except for his underpants which were hanging down. As the guests stepped in, they were met by this big bare arse. I don't know how long he'd been in the lift, going up and down like a fiddler's elbow. I don't think we were allowed back at that hotel.

The first time I was away with the team they played a trick on me. I went to my room after dinner to find they'd emptied it – the bed and all furniture gone, the room stripped.

I thought, do I ring the hotel manager and let him sort it out? But he might chuck us all out, which would be embarrassing for me, as a new manager. So I spent the night in Terry Burton's room. Next morning I found my bed several floors away and got one of the porters to move it back for a few quid.

Football teams have always done that sort of stuff. They did it in my day, going round the hotel's corridors changing all the shoes outside people's doors, or letting off fire extinguishers. These days, footballers have a much higher profile, so they have to be a bit more careful, especially when it comes to women. The single, younger lads, when they are away, are of course hoping to fill their boots, find as many women as they can. The senior, better known players know they are being watched.

We were in a hotel once, right on a beach, and there was this couple who were guests, who started sitting beside the team, by the pool or wherever, chatting to them. They turned out to be undercover reporters, using phoney names, trying to catch some of our players up to no good.

There were some topless birds on the beach, walking up and down, and of course the younger players were trying to chat them up. The senior players were not bothered – but one of the reporters snatched a photo of Dean Holdsworth, making it look as if he is talking to this topless bird. But he wasn't – and he'd just got married. They were also trying to catch Vinnie Jones eyeing the birds, but no luck there either.

We once got a call from an Italian TV programme, a sports show – they wanted to come and watch us training. I agreed, thinking it might be good publicity for us. They were coming to film for three days, with their presenter. About 10 o'clock on the first day, the presenter turns up with a big suitcase and asks if he could do a bit of training with us. He wanted to be in the shots in the background, while we were doing our warm-ups. So I says okay. He goes off to get changed – and turns up in big stupid shoes, like a clown's, and a fancy costume. He then stands in the background, making faces and doing a silly walk like Max Wall. I hadn't realized he was a comedian. Their plan was to take the piss out of the Crazy Gang, having heard we did silly things.

Well, our lads weren't going to stand for that, were they, having the piss taken. They let him fart about for 20 minutes, doing his silly walks, while they're doing their exercises, then they suddenly rushed and grabbed him. They stripped him naked, took him to a pile of stingy nettles and chucked him in. His film crew had to rush over and get him out. The last we saw of him he was slinking off the field with his suitcase, getting a taxi to the airport ...

EXCLUSIVE by JIM TAYLOR

CAPTAIN'S Log: Stardate 1971. The place: White Hart Lane, London.

Temperature: Sizzling and still rising!

Out on the field, young reserve player Graeme Souness is in Warp Factor 7. His Enterprising days as a Liverpool manager have yet to materialise.

And in the stands is a pretty teenager who also has a star future.

By 1993 Marina Sirtis would become a Porsche-driving Hollywood star, famous for her role as a sexy spacegirl in TV's Star Trek: The Next Generation.

But for the moment she has only one ambition: to be a Kling-on. And she is desperate to find a Spurs player she can Kling-on to.

And as Souness, now 40, faces a Spock of bother to keep his manager's job with Liverpool, Marina revealed another secret that will send the fiery Scot into hyper-drive.

She has confessed she only boldy went with Graeme to get closer to his team-mate Joe Kinnear, now the Wimbledon manager!

Ironically, Liverpool thrashed Spurs 6-2 yesterday in what could turn out to be Souness' last game in charge.

At the time of their relationship, Souness was young, fancy free and unmarried—and certainly not doing anything he was not supposed to.

But Marina, now 38, still looks back fondly at the man who took her to the stars and back.

She said: "You could say Graeme was my first love but up to then Joe was my heart-throb.

"I was really in love with him. Joe was lovely looking with blue eyes and dark hair. I had posters of him up on my wall along with the rest of the Spurs team.

Marina, who plays curvy counsellor Deanna Troi, in Star Trek, added: "I was one of those girls who hung around White Hart Lane to chat to the players.

"I didn't get to go out with Joe, to my dismay. So in the end I decided to go out with another player in the hope I'd get close to Joe.

Strict!

"I met Graeme at a supporters' club dance. I was 16 and he was 18. I got to know Graeme very well and we saw a lot of each other.

"My family are Greek and I had a very strict upbringing. My mother didn't want me having boyfriends but she'd let me watch Spurs play.

"I never told my mother about me and Graeme, although my brother Steve knew—I went up about 10 points in his estimation."

But Marina's love affair with the rising soccer star was doomed.

She said: "It all went wrong for us when Graeme was transferred to Middlesbrough.

"We didn't keep in touch. Graeme had a meteoric rise after his move and a fantastic career. I followed his progress and was happy with all his success.

"He's going through a bad time now and I feel sorry for him.

"I was shocked when I read about his triple heart by-pass surgery last year because he was always so fit.

"And now he looks liable to get a boot-mark on his behind this weekend at Liverpool."

Marina is now married to rock musician Michael Lamper and has a luxury Hollywood home.

But she says: "My skintight costumes on Star Trek are not nearly as revealing as the Spurs kit I once wore to a League Cup final.

"I was in micro-mini hotpants and a slinky Spurs shirt with No.2 on the back—'cos that was Joe Kinnear's number."

ANOTHER OUT OF THIS WORLD EXCLUSIVE

STARLET: Sexy Star Trek girl Marina first dated Souness to get close to his team mate Joe Kinnear

The newspaper with which the Wimbledon players covered the walls of the dressing-room – News of the World, *May 9, 1992*

They did have some fun with me now and again. I walked into the Wimbledon dressing room one day before a game to find they'd covered all the walls with pictures of me and some stunning actress. I was amazed. I didn't know who she was or what it was all about. Turned out there had been this story in the News of the World *in* which I was mentioned. They'd all rung each other up, over the weekend, bought about 10 copies each, come in early and plastered the walls with the pages.

'You dirty bastard, Gaffer, now we know your secret.' That's what they were all shouting at me as I came in. 'All those lies you've been telling us about you and your wife Bonnie. Now we know. The skeletons are coming out now, gaffer. You've been framed ...'

I looked at the photos on the wall, but still couldn't work it out as I hadn't seen the paper. Vinnie Jones, Robbie Earle and the others are still going 'Ooooh, oooh, naughty Joe'.

The story was about this girl who used to hang around Spurs when I was a young player. She'd bought a number 2 shirt and used to sleep in it – as it was the nearest she got to sleeping with me. One day she's in this pub talking to Graeme Souness, and I happened to come into the bar. Apparently she tried to get near me. I eventually said hello, and she told me she slept in my number 2 shirt.

That was the story. All new to me: I had no memory of this girl at all. A lot did hang around. Anyway, she later becomes an actress. She's now big in Hollywood. She stars in Star Trek. They were doing a big interview with her, as she'd won some award, and she came out with this story about following Spurs as a girl and fancying me.

I have seen her on the telly, since that story appeared. Very attractive dark-haired girl, Greek looking, called Marina Sintis. The lads all loved it, that some glamour bird had once fancied me.

We had some good laughs together. I always felt in tune with the players. I don't think there was ever a time when I felt unhappy at Wimbledon. But I did see some other managers having a hard time.

We were playing Villa at home in November 1994. We were 3-1 down with not long to go and Big Ron Atkinson is striding around in his smart suit, well chuffed with himself. I thought I'd just change a few things, see what might happen, nothing to lose, as we were so well behind. We get one goal back, then Vinnie scores, we get a fourth goal in the last minute, from Leonhardsen – and we won 4-3. A sensational match.

In the tunnel as we came off, I could see Ron's face. It was ashen.

He comes into my little room some time later and sits down, saying have you got a drink? I tell him I just drink lager after a match. He asks if I have any brandy. So I sent a waitress upstairs to get a bottle of brandy. He asks why I'm not upstairs, in the directors' lounge. I say I never go there. It does my head in, with all the guests there. People telling me what to do and what not to do, what went wrong and why. I don't need all that. I'll go up later, when it's just Sam left.

Ron sits there with the bottle of brandy and his head in his hands saying, 'Fucking hell, that's it, fucking hell, this is the end. What a team I've got, what a defence, that's it, I'm finished ...'

I says come on Ron, we all feel rotten after a defeat. I've had enough of them. You've got to take it. He says no, it's not like that, this is the end. Eventually he got on the team coach back to Villa.

I thought he's just having a bad day. Then, next day he gets the sack. Just shows you what a cruel game football is. You're winning 3-1, then you lose and bang goes your job.

But I have to say I never got in that situation. There was no game which everybody was saying would have to be won, or that would be the end of me. I felt no pressure about the actual job. Just the pressures of doing it, which got harder and more stressful all the time ...

Chapter Thirty

Bonnie was naturally pleased that Joe was making such a success of managing Wimbledon. But what she had feared, right from the beginning, came true very quickly.

'He finished that first season, 1991-92, on a high. So that was good. He'd got what he wanted, and was obviously suited to it, and Sam and all the players loved him. But my God, from then on, it was terrible. He never switched off. He was out first thing every morning and not back till very late at night, then he'd just sit there, watching videos, not coming to bed sometimes till four in the morning.

'The strain was unbelievable. If it was a live match, and I wasn't there, I'd watch his face on TV. I'd see it go white and him ageing about 10 years in 90 minutes. After every game, it would take him three hours to wind down and look semi-normal.

'Even then, all weekend, he'd still be going over the match in his head, or talking to people about it. Not with me. He never discussed a game with me. Women don't talk about football. In 30 years of football, I still don't know how grown men can discuss the same match for four hours solid. Just one game. Incredible.

'But Wimbledon are a very nice club. I was made to feel part of a family. Over the years, I did visit all the other Premier League clubs, and I have to say no other club treated a manager's wife as well as Wimbledon. They don't invite you into their boardroom, the way Wimbledon does. Mind you, a lot of managers' wives probably wouldn't want to be invited. But at

Wimbledon, Sam and his wife treated me as part of their own family, not as the wife of an employee.

'Over the years, I met a lot of very interesting people through Wimbledon, from Rod Stewart to Tony Blair. Tony Blair came to a game when he became Labour leader. I discussed with him his job and Joe's job, about the respective stresses and responsibilities. I also met ambassadors, visiting heads of state. People from all walks of life are interested in football these days, so Sam or someone would meet them and invite them into the director's box.

'As the manager's wife, I had no connection with the players of course. They don't want you hanging around. You have to keep your distance. Joe was more on their wavelength than many managers, and would sometimes go out with them for a lads' night out, but he tried to keep his distance, keep their respect as the gaffer.

'There were occasions when a player's wife might ring up, and I would answer the phone, and they'd be moaning about their husband being left out of the team. I would never have done that when Joe was at Spurs. Imagine ringing Bill Nick to complain! So I kept out of all those sort of things.

'All that worried me was Joe, the toll it was taking on his health. He never put on weight in Dubai, which was strange, as it was a fairly easy life. Perhaps it was with not socializing after games when he was out there. But at Wimbledon, I could see his weight shooting up almost from the time he became manager. It wasn't just that he was eating and drinking more, which he was, but he was taking no exercise and generally having a ridiculous lifestyle.

'I used to think that with someone so involved, something is bound to go wrong, something will break. He would push himself to the limit.

'Of course I told him to slow down, take it easy, take more exercise. I warned him all the time. And he'd say don't nag, as all men do. I couldn't break into his total commitment. He is a passionate person, very volatile. And he didn't want to break out of his way of working, his style of management.

'The rewards were wonderful, financially and in other ways. He got well paid. I could buy designer clothes. We had nice holidays in the Caribbean. We met lots of famous people, got invited everywhere. Joe became well known, recognized most places we went. Everyone liked him. Good old Joe.

'But I kept on thinking, how much longer can he keep this up? Something will have to give in the end. And what happened was – something happened to me. Not to Joe, which is what I had been expecting.

'It was in 1997, towards the end of the season, after Wimbledon had got beaten in the semi-final of the Cup by Chelsea. Joe had set his heart on going to Wembley. He'd been four times as a player, and won them all, and his fantasy was to lead out his own team at Wembley. His disappointment was total.

'As a result, my hair started to fall out. I didn't understand at first that there was any connection. When it began, I thought it's glands, or a skin complaint. I was wrongly diagnosed at first, till a specialist told me it was stress related. I'd obviously been worried about Joe, hit by his disappointment.

'For almost a year, I hardly went out. I wouldn't face the world. I didn't want to talk about it, or have anyone looking at me. I know Joe is not exactly a household face, but at the sort of places we went to, people always recognized him. Those were the people I didn't want looking at me. I imagined they would be staring at me. I thought about getting a wig, but decided against it.

'A friend tried to get me out of it, saying you're not dying, you haven't got cancer, come on, get a grip. Joe said that's it, you're not coming to Wimbledon any more. I had been helping to entertain, looking after people in the boardroom. He said don't get involved; just leave me to worry about my job.

'Anyway, after a year, my hair started to grow again. Now I've got over it. That's why I can talk about it.

'But it was strange, getting so stressed about Joe's job. And yet that season had been a success. They'd got to two semi-finals, which was very good for Wimbledon, and they ended up 8th in the Premiership, which was very respectable.

'We all of course react differently to things. It had clearly not happened to me overnight. It had been building up inside me over several years. That was just the way it had come out.

'I still worried about Joe, of course. Wondering if and when and how something would happen to him.'

Chapter Thirty-one

For our evening match on Wednesday, 3 March 1999, against Sheffield Wednesday, we travelled up the day before, as we usually did. Those living to the south of London reported to Wimbledon's training ground where they parked their cars and got on the team coach. People like me, living in the north of London, John Hartson, Carl Cort, Mick Hartford, David Kemp and several others, joined the coach at the Watford Hilton Hotel, to save us dragging all through London.

On arrival in Sheffield, we went to our hotel to check in then did some light training in the afternoon on one of the university's football pitches. Just an hour, going over various set routines. Next morning, on the Wednesday, we did some more light training, a little loosening up. It was really to get a breath of fresh air. Footballers hate being cooped up in a hotel for hour after hour before a match.

After lunch, mainly pasta all round, we still had several hours to put in. The players were supposed to be resting in their rooms. I got this knock on my bedroom door and was given a message from Prince Naseem. I had met him once before, in Dublin, but I didn't know he was in the hotel. He'd rigged up a ring in one of the conference rooms and was training for a world title fight. He invited us all to come and watch him have a workout. So we all went down to see him.

He was punching this huge training bag, dancing in front of it, throwing punches at lightning speed. It was incredible. All of us were amazed that he could move and punch so fast. It was great watching him, gave us something interesting to do while we hung around.

About four o'clock, all the players went back to their rooms, supposedly to have a snooze or at least a lie down. When I got to my room, I felt a touch of heartburn. I often got it, caused by all the stupid late-night eating I was doing. But it wasn't serious. Not bad enough to take a Rennie.

I held the pre-match team-talk in one of the suites in the hotel, about 5.30. I had my board and wrote things on it. It was mainly the usual stuff – reminding them of their set plays, what each player was meant to do, their positions at corners. One or two set routines were changed, as we knew Wednesday had been watching us a lot.

I felt fine, fit and well, no aches or pains, well and fit as I normally was for the age of 52. Yeah, I'd put on weight, everyone was always on at me about it. Rival supporters would shout things at me about being a 'fat bastard'. I could take that.

For years and years, I'd been around 11 stone, 4 ounces, a reasonable weight for someone 5′ 8″ tall. But with forever travelling round the country, eating at funny times, my weight had gradually crept up. By March 1999, I was over 15 and a half stone. Okay, 16 stone.

Bonnie had nagged at me, but I'd never seriously tried to get it down. I did eat salads, which she made for me, to balance my diet, but I was always sneaking other meals, all day long. I would have tea and toast for breakfast at home, all very sensible, then a second breakfast when I got to work, a big fry-up in the transport caff, in the days when we had one at the training ground.

After training, I'd race to an afternoon game in the London area, say to watch Chelsea reserves. Then I'd drive to an evening game, which might be anywhere. On the way, I'd stop somewhere and have a Big Mac and chips. I didn't normally drive myself, so that wasn't a pressure. I usually went with our chief scout Ron Suite or with Sam, Kempey or Mick, who loves driving. I'm not a car enthusiast.

We'd have hospitality at the evening match, in the boardroom, where I'd stuff my face, but I wouldn't drink. I never drink in the boardrooms of other clubs. I always think that looks bad. I always stuck to a coffee. But I might have a lager elsewhere, in the players' lounge. Then on the way home, I would stop for another Big Mac and chips. Stuff like that, any old junk food.

On Saturdays, after an away match, I'd come home very late and bring in fish and chips which I'd buy on the way home. Bonnie would have videoed Match of the Day for me, so I'd sit and watch it into the early hours, on my own, eating the fish and chips.

After home matches, that was very different. Bonnie and I and Sam and his wife usually went up West for a meal, places like Quaglinos in Mayfair. We'd start with oysters and pink champagne at the bar, sitting there drinking, still going over the match. It does take a long time to get it out of your head.

About 10.30, we'd sit down in the restaurant and have a full meal. Smoked salmon perhaps to start, followed by steak, that sort of stuff, and wine of course, the best Fleurie. So yes, I had got into the habit of eating too much generally, and also at funny times of the day. But no, I didn't feel unwell or unhealthy.

I was the second longest serving manager in the Premiership, after Alex Ferguson. I felt totally confident as Wimbledon's manager after nine years with the club. We'd got to three semis in the last two years – in the FA Cup and League Cup in 1996-97, being beaten by Chelsea and Leicester. Earlier in the 1998-99 season we'd got knocked out of the League Cup semi again, by Spurs this time. So we'd done well, for a small club. I felt fully supported by Sam. I can honestly say I didn't feel any work pressures.

When I did get the occasional indigestion, a bit of burping and heartburn, it didn't really worry me at all. I knew it was just too many chips and burgers, that was all. Taking a few Rennies, that usually cured it.

But that evening, 3 March, on the coach to the ground, I felt myself coming over all sweaty, which was most unusual. I was soon mopping my brow. One of the team coaches, David Kemp, noticed what was happening and asked if I was okay. I said fine fine, just feels a bit hot on this coach.

In the dressing room at Hillsborough, Mick Harford remarked

on how pale I looked, but again I just shrugged it off. 'It's my poxy heartburn,' I said. 'And I think I might be getting flu as well.' I asked Steve Allen, the club's physio, for a couple of Rennies which I then took.

I went out on to the pitch for the warm-up with the team, just to have a look at the surface, discuss what sort of studs should be worn.

As I was walking off the pitch, going down the tunnel, I started to gulp. My throat sort of went funny. I was having trouble breathing. Fucking hell, I thought, what's this? My chest was all heavy and I felt pins and needles in my left arm. I tried to shake it out but it was sort of going numb. I could feel myself staggering.

Steve, the physio, and Joe Dillon, the kitman, took hold of me. They both said I was looking dreadful. One of them ran off to fetch the Sheffield Wednesday doctor. The others walked me into the Wednesday treatment room. Their doc arrived, looked in my eyes, took my shirt off, got his stethoscope out and checked my chest. He pressed my left hand and asked if I could feel it. I said no, I can feel nothing.

'Joe,' he says, 'you're showing all the signs of going through a heart attack.'

He then got out a needle and gave me an injection, firing some adrenaline stuff into my side. He then put an oxygen mask on my face and turned on the taps from an oxygen tank. Two ambulance men arrived and got me on a stretcher and wheeled me down the corridor. They were going like the clappers, racing down the corridor, and put me straight into their ambulance. Our kitman, Joe, came with me in the ambulance.

I was semi-conscious, by then. I couldn't speak anyway because of the oxygen mask on my face. This paramedic woman held my hand and kept saying, 'You're doing okay.' I just nodded, being unable to talk. I could hear the ambulance's siren wailing as we raced through the streets of Sheffield. Is this it? I was saying to myself. Is this the end? Or am I having a nightmare?

At the Northern General Hospital, they wheeled me straight off into an operating theatre where there was a whole team ready, all the surgeons and nurses in masks, waiting for me. They set up drips, wired my chest to lots of instruments and machines. I could hear this bleep, bleep, bleep. I thought if it stops, if it just misses one bleep, that's me, I'm a gonner ...

The main surgeon gave me an injection of streptokinase. I think that's the name. He said it was a clot buster. I was having a coronary, right in the middle of it, but they'd got to me early on. The next hour would be crucial, he said. He asked if there was anyone I wanted him to ring. Anyone I needed to be in touch with right now.

That was worrying. It was like my last will and testament. My chance to give my last words, before I went. I knew that Sam had already rung Bonnie. I reckoned she was probably on her way. There didn't seem any point in ringing her. Or anyone. So I said no thanks. I don't need to ring anybody ...

That hour was the worst hour I've ever spent. They all went out and I just lay there, trying to work it out. The phone offer had worried me. And them saying that the next hour was crucial. I started counting it out in seconds – one, two, three, four, five, six ... Then I started counting the seconds backwards – 60, 59, 58, 57. Anything to make the time go quickly. But it wouldn't.

I was wishing every minute away, but every minute seemed like years. I felt drowsy, but I didn't want to go to sleep. I could do nothing. It was all out of my control. I didn't know what the hell my body was doing. I just had to lie there and wait.

After an hour, they all came back in. They did more tests, took my pulse, checked everything. They said things seemed to be under control, how they wanted them. But the next 48 hours would still be vital. They'd put me in intensive care, keep checking me.

I was wheeled out into a private room, passing room after room of people who'd also had heart attacks. I hadn't realized I was in a specialized heart attack department. It was full of people like me, fighting for their lives.

Bonnie arrived, and my mother and my sisters visited me as well. After a few days, I was allowed up for a bit. They gave me breathing exercises to do. I slowly started to do little walks round the hospital. Then I had to climb up stairs to get my stamina back. Two nurses seemed to be with me all the time. And of course there were endless tests going on.

Danny Wilson, Wednesday's manager, came to see me. He told me how well my lads had done. Wimbledon had won the game 2-1 and gone 5th in the league. I had never thought of asking, not during that evening, not when it happened. I was expecting the worst, convinced I was dying. I wasn't thinking about football.

Chapter Thirty-two

Looking back, Bonnie thinks she saw signs of stress earlier in the season. 'I'd been ill for a start, and been rushed into hospital for tests. Luckily there was nothing wrong with me, but it was a worrying time for both of us.

'Then Wimbledon got beaten by Spurs in the semi-final of the League Cup. Wimbledon had played so well all season, and I think they were about 6th in the league at the time. But that day, 16 February it was, they lost to Spurs 1-0 in the second leg of the semi. They just had an off day. Joe was devastated, heartbroken. He'd wanted to beat Spurs so much, because you know he loves them, and get to Wembley at long last.

'The fateful trip to Sheffield was only two weeks later. I do think they were connected. Things had been coming to a head inside Joe. He had rung me, when he arrived in Sheffield, from the team hotel. All he said was how cold it was, he was freezing.

'I was out somewhere in the early evening. I came in about seven o'clock and listened to the phone messages. There was one from Sam. I could hear his voice, but he'd left no message. I thought that's funny, Sam ringing me, when a match is just about to begin. Most unusual, but I didn't really think much about it.

'Then a bit later, Dave Barnard [Wimbledon's chief executive] rang me. He said Joe wasn't well. He'd been taken to hospital as a precaution, but not to worry. I knew what it must be. Joe's had a heart attack. Please God, I thought, make him okay.

'I went sort of numb. I rang the hospital every 40 minutes, but I just couldn't take it all in. The phone never stopped ringing. But I didn't want to talk to anyone. Russelle, my daughter, came round. I thought of going up to Sheffield, that night, but I couldn't face driving up the M1, and I didn't want to be driven. I got the train times to Sheffield, but I couldn't face the train. I just went numb. I rang the hospital all the time, but I did nothing.

'Next morning, I did get the train to Sheffield. Joe was in intensive care, all wired up. I had never expected to see Joe look like that. All my life with him, 30 years, he'd been so vibrant, so volatile. Now he seemed to have been emptied. I could see he was scared, something I had never witnessed before.

'The staff were brilliant, so helpful and kind. Everyone was incredible. I stayed up there for the two weeks, moved into a hotel, while waiting for Joe to recover.

'The press were awful. They were trying to con their way to his bedside to get pictures, pretending they were hospital staff, or visiting other patients. I thought it was obscene.

'On the other hand, there were hundreds of cards from well-wishers, masses of fruit, so many flowers, arriving all the time. I was overwhelmed. I just had not realized how Joe was known and loved by so many people. A "Regular Joe", I suppose. That's how people saw him.'

Sam Hammam says he saw no signs at all of Joe being under stress at the time and certainly did not expect him to have a heart attack. 'It never came into my mind. Joe worked hard, but I expect all my managers to work hard.'

But Sam was less cheerful at the time about the way the team was performing. It is true that in January they had climbed to 6th, but after that things had not gone so well.

'The reason I'd bought Hartson was to throw everything into the pot that I could, use all our resources, in order at last to climb into the top three. That was something we had never achieved. Getting in the top three would get us into Europe. So that was the aim. But Hartson didn't play well and Ainsworth, the other new purchase, got injured. From January to March, the team had lost a bit of confidence. So there was pressure on Joe, as there was on all of us. But just the usual sorts of pressures you have in football.

'So I was very surprised by Joe's collapse. I stayed at the hospital with him in Sheffield that night. I was by his bedside most of the time, then when Bonnie came next day, I went home.

'While he was recovering, I never spoke to him once about the club. Or about football. I kept off all that. I just wanted him to get better. He is my buddy, my friend. I love him.'

Chapter Thirty-three

I was upset by what the newspapers were doing. Two of the Sunday papers were offering money for the first photo of me in the hospital, lying in my bed. Or they wanted the first photo of me when I came out, me with nurses, saying thank you. The offers were going up all the time, £10,000, £15,000, for exclusive photos. I told them all to get lost. I wasn't having any of it.

It seemed sort of unsavoury, distasteful. It would be an insult to all the other heart attack victims lying there, if I made some money out of my heart attack and my treatment.

It leaked out that I would leave on a certain day, but I actually left three days earlier, sneaking out quickly by a side entrance. I'd been in for two weeks before they thought I was fit enough to go home. The main doctor was brilliant, I am so grateful to him.

I managed to walk out, with the help of a walking stick. I said thanks to all the staff, who'd been wonderful, then Bonnie and I got driven home. Mr Richards, Wednesday's chairman, arranged for a chauffeur to drive us down to London.

I went straight to bed when I got home. For the next few weeks I just rested at home. Gradually, I began to walk round the garden. It's a very long garden.

I had to take lots of tablets and do some light exercises. I had my own fitness trainer. She came every day at first to help me. I was put on a strict diet of course. No alcohol at all. In a few weeks I'd lost one and a half stones.

NOT DON FOR JUST YET!

JOE GETS BOOKED AGAIN ... *Kinnear enjoys a bit of reading*   Pictures: DAVID NEW

Sunday People, *March 28, 1999: Joe recovers at home.*

The first day I went out on my own it was in trepidation. I walked down our street and into the grounds of Mill Hill public school. They have a few little hills in their grounds. I thought I'd chance going up one. I managed it, breathing heavily, blowing like a billie goat. I thought of trying another hill, then thought no, don't push it.

But soon I was going up and down the little hill six times. When I had the slightest stitch, or any tummy upset, or any sort of pain in my chest, then I worried, which I still do. Suppose I always will. But that's to be expected.

I take one aspirin a day and one pill called Atenol which is a clot buster. I also carry a little spray thing. If I ever get that feeling again, of being unable to breathe, then I have to use it. It's a sort of kick-start, giving you instant oxygen. I think that's it. I carry it whenever I'm going out, just in case. Of course I haven't used it yet. I'd be in a bad way, wouldn't I, if I did have to use it.

I had loads of tests for months after the heart attack. Dr Jackson

185

at the London Bridge Hospital, their top heart man, was looking after me, giving me things like stress tests. They stick you on a machine, put about ten wires on your body, then you run. They can slow it down, speed it up, make it as if you're running up an incline. It all goes into a computer, then out comes this big sheet of paper. They read it saying, 'Pulse, yes very good, heart, excellent, well done, blood pressure, very good.' They make you feel as if you've just completed a marathon. I've done five of those tests. Passed them all.

The most amazing test I had was something called an angiogram. They shave round your privates then cut a hole in your groin. You're wide awake as they just use a local anaesthetic. Then they shove in a camera which goes up into your stomach and has a look at your heart.

I'm lying there in this theatre, flat out on the bed, and above my head are all the TV monitors, showing my heart. Really scary. The camera moves round, so you see it from different angles. The doctor explains it all, what it all means. He told me the heart is like a tree, with all these branches coming off it. You can see them, all the valves and stuff.

Then they pumped me full of a red dye. You can feel it going in. It feels hot, and you feel a bit sick, but it's not painful. You see it going round your body, on the TV screen, see your veins filling up. They can stop it, at any stage, to examine it.

I could actually see the dye getting to the bit where I'd had my blockage – and I watched it flow through. It didn't even slow down. Just went straight through. I didn't really understand all the terms and medical stuff, but I followed most of it. I learned a lot in fact. That test took six hours and in the end Dr Jackson said, 'Perfect, perfect.'

Today's technology is amazing, but then it is with everything, not just the heart. When I was a player, if you had a cartilage op, you could be off for six months. Now they're playing again in three weeks. When I had my broken leg, I was out for over 12 months. Now it's half that time. Repairing your heart is just the same – better and faster today.

They explained to me what the heart does – how it's the body's engine room, but it needs the proper fuel to run the body. I was eating all the wrong fuel. All those late-night fish and chips on the motorway. I used to know every Little Chef on every motorway between London and Scotland.

I now know that all those chips, beans and eggs and stuff were lying on my stomach when I went to bed. The acid builds up and eventually gets to the heart. Then I used to drink pints of Guinness, pints of lager, no problems. I now know all those are fattening. Then driving all round the country like a maniac.

But the doctors have told me that no one single thing causes a heart attack, it's a combination. The skinniest people can have heart attacks and die. We had a neighbour, aged 52, not at all fat. He spent the afternoon gardening, came in, had a meal and was watching television. His wife went out to make him a cup of tea – when she came back, he was dead. Heart attack, killed him in minutes, just like that.

They say stress is a cause, but what's stress? I didn't think I suffered from it. The only time I got seriously aggravated was during a match, but that's part and parcel of football. You scream and shout on the touchline for 90 minutes, trying to get your instructions over. It did knacker my voice box. Even on a Monday, I would come to training and still feel my throat sore. But that was the only ill effect I could see with the sort of work I was doing.

Then of course the enormous highs, the pleasure when we beat Man. Utd or one of the other big clubs. That made up for everything. No stress there, mate. Champagne all round in the boardroom, then a slap-up meal in the West End. Very good for stress, all that.

While I was recovering, I was given a dietician, who told me what to eat from now on. And I've stuck to it. Well, almost all of it. I kept off the alcohol for a whole six months. I'm now on to the occasional glass of red wine or glass of champagne in company. But the Guinness and lager have gone for good. I never drank spirits. Fleurie and Brouilly, those are my best tickles now.

Now that the six months are up, I have put back on a bit of weight, just a few pounds. I think I'm now 14 stone, but the doctor says I'm fit and well. My waist had gone up to 40″, after years of being only 32″. Now it's about 35″. Look, me trousers are falling off me!

All I really have to do from now on is watch my diet. I've given up all fats. We don't have butter any more. We have something called Benecol. Gawd knows what it is, but it's low cholesterol. That's me from now on – bye-bye sausages. Fish and chips have been kicked into touch; bacon is out of the window.

I know I was lucky. If it had happened on the motorway some-where, which it might well have done, I would have been a gonner. Or even here at home. It happened where a doctor was right on hand and I reached a specialist hospital in minutes and got brilliant attention. Yes, I was bloody lucky.

I now consider myself totally recovered, mentally and physically.

Chapter Thirty-four

'Joe was a good boy, when he came home,' says Bonnie. 'He did lose weight, stuck to his diet. He was excellent. The mental thing was harder to recover from. He lacked confidence for so long, frightened by every little twinge in his body, or his heart. Or he imagined there were twinges.

'It did make him take stock of his life, being given that terrible warning. He did see there was much more to life than football. He spent a lot of time playing with our grandson Nicholas, and he really enjoyed it. Then we had a good holiday together in Portugal when he was up to travelling.

'In theory there is now no need for him to have another heart attack. He knows how to live and how to avoid it. It's up to him.

'In the last few weeks, he's been a bit naughtier. He's got rid of his personal trainer. His diet is fine, no complaints there, but he's not running, sorry jogging. And I know he has a glass or two when he goes to Ireland for the TV work. You know what they're like in Ireland, once he gets together with his old Irish footballing colleagues.

'I do beg him to take more exercise – and of course get told off for nagging. But healthwise, he has perfectly recovered. Losing another stone would help even more, but I'm pleased by what he's done. Physically, I think he's in good shape, as safe as any of us are. He's now joined a tennis club.

'As for going back to football, that's up to him. But knowing him, I think he misses it too much. He's lost without it. I'd prefer it if he found a media career, and he's had so many offers, but he says he doesn't want that.'

As Joe slowly recovered, Sam left any decision up to him, not wanting to put any pressure on him.

'After three months,' says Sam, 'I could see he was physically better. So that was a great relief. My worry had been that he would tell me one day that he was fine – but that the doctors had said he should never return to football management. That was my fear.

'My other fear was if I get Joe back, what do I get? Will he be the same man, the same manager? Will he no longer want to do things like scouting and travelling? But all I wanted was for him to return, on any conditions.

'I made no changes at the club. I did nothing, prepared to wait till he was ready to come back. Mick Hartford and David Kemp were put in temporary charge. But only till Joe returned. That was made clear. Joe would return. My Joe, the Joe I love. I would not have put them in charge, if I had thought Joe was not coming back. I would have looked for a new manager. So as the months went on, I waited for Joe to tell me the date when he would be returning ...'

Chapter Thirty-five

Mental recovery, well that was a longer process than the physical aspect – trying to think things out, what was I going to do with the rest of my life.

When I was lying there in the Sheffield hospital for those two weeks, wired up, with the bloody bleep-bleep going, I was making vows. If I get out of this, I told myself, it means I've had a tap on the shoulder. Someone's telling me I am human.

You go through life thinking not me, it won't happen to me. So I lay there making all these resolutions to be a better person, to devote myself to Bonnie, my children, my mother, my sisters. There is more to life than football, so I was thinking. Yet all I've done with my life is dedicate it to football, 35 wonderful but tough years. That's got to change.

It was all to do with trying to stop myself having negative thoughts, which of course I was having at the same time, listening to the bleeps. I could still cop it, I might not yet recover. I might not be able to do anything, if I do recover. So I'm telling myself what a wiser, better person I'm going to be from now on, if I get out of this.

Yet strangely enough, I never actually said to myself that's it, I'm finished with football. I might have thought I won't devote myself to it as much in future, spend more time with the family, be a better person, but I never thought I'm not going back to football.

The minute I had the strength, I was quizzing the doctors, asking them just to estimate. I wouldn't hold them to it. I just wanted them to guess if it would be months or even years, before I could be back at work. They all said they wouldn't be able to tell for six months. Then we'd see.

My real fear was that they would say yes, you will recover – but you must never go back to football. I dreaded that, but they never said it. They said it's up to me. If I want to go back to football, that's fine. I just have to watch my diet.

It's true that Sam put no pressure on me. He just told me what he'd always told me – that I had a job for life. I could become a consultant, anything I wanted. He would never sack me.

The team didn't do so well under Mick and David. In fact they hardly won again for the rest of the season. We were 6th, at the time of my collapse, after beating Sheffield Wednesday, but we ended up 16th.

Sam was getting concerned. So was I. I worried about Wimbledon FC. I always have done. So we began to think that the club couldn't really hang on six months, till I was fit again. We began to think about what was best for Wimbledon FC.

In my mind, I'd always thought I'd give Wimbledon 10 years as manager. I wouldn't leave before then, I'd told Sam that. But after 10 years, I'll start thinking about going to a bigger club. I won't apply, or do anything about it, but I'll be open to offers. I'm sure Sam understood that. But of course I'd never thought of me collapsing. That wasn't the way I wanted it to end. But that had changed everything.

As I'm sitting around thinking, getting all my strength back, thinking about my life, my future, I realized I had in fact done 10 years at Wimbledon since arriving there in 1989 – eight as manager and the two years before as a coach. I decided that my heart attack was a sign, telling me it was time to move on.

So I told Sam. I said I wouldn't be coming back as manager. We'd call it a day. I know I'd promised him 10 years as manager, and I'd nearly done that, but events had intervened. I hadn't planned to have a heart attack, had I? I said let's call it quits. They should start looking for a new manager now.

I didn't know what else I would do. Nothing definite had happened, but I wouldn't come back. I just wanted to leave, take stock, decide about the rest of my life.

Sam said what about another two years? I said no. He said what about staying on as consultant, while they found a new manager? I didn't fancy that. I don't want the sort of job David Pleat has at Spurs, stuck in an office all the time, not working with players.

Sam said I must not do anything rash. I must think about it longer. He'd give me another week, in case I changed my mind. But I said no, my mind is made up. It was the hardest decision of my life.

We discussed who might be a likely new manger. David Platt's name came up. We discussed him. He seemed the right age and capability. We didn't worry about what had gone wrong with his short spell as a manager in Italy. He was still very young. I suppose the only thing we did worry about with him was the example of Peter Withe. When you've been a player at the top, played for England and all that, had experience of big clubs, then Wimbledon is a bit of a jolt. The Crazy Gang is not like other clubs. You have to appreciate that. So we worried that Platty might be like Withe, not able to understand the Wimbledon mentality.

The club had been sold by now to the Norwegians. This happened well before my heart attack. Sam had been looking for some years for someone to put money into the club. It had been a struggle for him all those years, taking all the strain, balancing the books, and getting harder all the time. In order to survive, we had to get stronger and richer. If you can't compete with the big boys, you go backwards.

When I became Wimbledon manager, I had half a million to spend on players. I thought I was very lucky, as if I'd won the pools. But that was back in 1992. Today, David O'Leary must have about £30 million to spend – but he's saying it's not enough.

Wimbledon has been the David to the Goliaths of the Premier League, permanently surprising everyone. But it can't go on. Even clubs who are much bigger than us now have little chance of doing what Wimbledon has done, of getting to where we are. Birmingham City, Manchester City, Wolves, Charlton, and several others get bigger crowds than Wimbledon, have a bigger stadium, which they own, and their own training ground. They have more potential than us – but they've either failed to come up, or failed to stay up. We've done it, while owning very little and getting crowds of only 10,000. Who's going to be the next Wimbledon? Nobody.

So Sam had to find more money. That's when the Norwegians came along. The main man has got millions, in fishing fleets, property, land, paper, God knows what. He's huge. They invited us over to Norway, me and Sam, when the deal was being discussed. We went in their private helicopter all over Norway and saw things like reindeer. I didn't actually believe in reindeers. I thought they were made up, like Santa Claus. The two Norwegians seemed okay, businessmen rather than football people, but very nice. They paid Sam £35 million and got 80 per cent of the club. Everyone was very pleased. They didn't interfere at all in the running of the club, not when I was still there.

Life went on the same way. At some clubs, the ones that are PLCs, the manager gets a written notification of a board meeting two months ahead. For years at Wimbledon, the meetings were usually just me and Sam, perhaps meeting at a local caff. I'd say I want to buy so and so and he'd say yes, he could get the money, or no he couldn't. If he said yes, I left all the money arrangements to him. Even when the Norwegians took over, it went on much the same. Sam looked after the finances. I ran the team.

But when I fell ill, then the Norwegians did get worried. If you think about it, what they had really bought was me. They weren't buying a stadium or a training ground. All they were buying was a team with a manager – and it was the team I had created. In selling to them, Sam had been able to assure them that I was staying. I'd promised him those 10 years.

Now of course they got worried, when I decided I was leaving. They had been upset when I was ill, disappointed by the poor results, but now they had to do something.

I think it was them who came up with the idea of Egil Olsen as the new manager. Sam asked me what I thought and I said it sounded good. Being Norwegian, they would know who he was and be able to talk to him. He had good international knowledge as he'd done well as Norway's national coach. But he hadn't got any knowledge of the Premier League. That could be a handicap.

The problem with Wimbledon, which we could all see clearly

enough, is that you have to make the next step up. You can't stand still, otherwise you end up going backwards. In my eight years, we'd got to two FA Cup semi-finals and been 6th in the Premiership. To reach the next stage, or even just keep Wimbledon in the top half, you need millions, or else you'll be struggling, then find yourself in the First Division.

In my first few years at Wimbledon, I built a defence which had cost practically nothing. Warren Barton cost just £250,000. Then we sold him for a fortune. Next time round, I had to pay a lot more – £750,000 for Kenny Cunningham. £1.9 million for Ben Thatcher. The prices were going up all the time, but they were still bargains. They are now worth fortunes as well. But it can't go on. I can't work miracles for ever.

Next time, I don't want to do all that scratching around in the lower divisions and non-league, looking for cheap bargains, then working on them. I would like to be at a club where I can think of making an offer for Ronaldo not someone from Brentford reserves. I've done all that.

It doesn't have to be one of the top clubs. I'm not expecting to go to Manchester United, Arsenal or Chelsea. I just want a club with potential, which perhaps has been good in the past, which now has got some money to spend and has strong ambition. I'd love the chance to recreate their glory days for them. That's my fantasy, that's what I'd like to happen in an ideal world.

If I was, say, manager of Spurs, I wouldn't be looking at Brentford reserves. Spurs fans want the best, because they have had the best. They remember Jimmy Greaves and Dave Mackay and they want those sort of players again. They don't want Joe Soap from Exeter.

I don't know if I would succeed with money to spend. I've never had it. But I'd like to have a go. We all know money is not a guarantee of anything, but it's a help.

I had 10 years playing with a top club. I had 10 years at Wimbledon, keeping them in the top division. Now I'd like another 10 years with a club I could turn into a top club, the way Peter Reid has done with Sunderland. We all knew their potential.

So, that was how my mind was running, that's why I decided to pack it in at Wimbledon. I didn't say all this to Sam. I didn't want to say I've done with Wimbledon, I'm fed up with Wimbledon. Because that wouldn't be quite true. I still love Wimbledon. In whatever number of years I've got left in football, I just want a different challenge.

I agreed a leaving deal with Sam and Wimbledon. They kept paying my wages, during the six months I was recovering. Then they agreed I would get a loyalty bonus of £500,000.

I left not knowing if I was ever going to be able to work again. Some people might not want to employ me, knowing I'd had a heart attack. Would they be able to trust my health? Would I? We shall see.

Chapter Thirty-six

It all came as a shock to Sam Hammam, so he says. He just hadn't expected Joe would decide to leave.

'At the end of the season, in May, I was thinking of plans for next season, things like details of pre-season training arrangements. It looked as if he would be back for next season.

'Then he asked to come and see me for a meeting, at my house. He sat on the couch, where you are sitting now along with David Barnard the chief executive. And it appears he's thinking of leaving!

'I could not believe it. I still don't understand it. I never will. I began to think he's already had an offer, which will be official in a few weeks. I thought it might be Celtic, as that was the press rumour at the time. They are a big club, who can pay big money. From our conversation, it seemed to me that that was the main attraction – Joe now wanted to go to a bigger club.

'His heart attack had not just had a physical effect but a mental one, making him, so I began to think, dissatisfied with Wimbledon. He never used to be, as far as I could see. He didn't seem the sort to be interested in things like a million-a-year salary, or two million, or whatever it was he appeared to have got into his mind.

'I always considered that Joe was highly paid. He earned £500,000 a year – which cost us more like £600,000 a year with his car and other things.

'He's probably told you about the various fines he had from the FA over the years, banned for swearing at refs and fined

£20,000. Who do you think paid those fines? The club paid. Who paid for him to have a chauffeur drive him everywhere when he lost his licence? We did.

'I'm just telling you this to show you why I think he was well rewarded. We didn't begrudge it – he had done well for us. Then so had Dave Bassett. So had Bobby Gould, winning the FA Cup. Joe got us twice into 6th position, and to several semis, so he had done exceptionally well. And I like to think we all got along excellently. He never came and asked for a rise in all those 10 years. I was the one who put his money up, without him asking. He was on full salary, for those six months he was recovering, while he decided what to do.

'So here he is, appearing to me to be after more money, somewhere else. That's how it seemed, how his mind was running. Was he after more money for himself, and more money to spend? That would be natural I suppose, though I'd hate it as I wanted my Joe to stay.'

Sam, it was never the money, I found myself saying in Joe's defence. He wanted a chance to run a different sort of club, with different sorts of problems. To test himself elsewhere. After all, he's now 53, he hasn't got many management years left. Time for one last change. Joe told me he had always planned to give 10 years to Wimbledon, which he had done.

'I never knew that. That's news to me.

'Anyway, it's a fantasy, this thing about going to a bigger club and having more money to spend. Go to a bigger club and you are sacked in six months and you are out of a job. What use is that? Joe had a job for life here. I would never have sacked him.

'It's true we could never pay him one million or two million at Wimbledon, but he was stupid to think that he could go somewhere else and be happier than he was here. I told him that. I argued with him. But I couldn't make him see what he had at Wimbledon.

'You are a married man? Right. You might think it will be nice to have three nights sleeping with Claudia, what is she called, Shiffer is it, or three nights with let's say, the Duchess of York ...'

Hold on. Let's not go quite so over the top.

'You might think that, many men would, but one of the many virtues which God gives us is contentment. You have chosen your wife, a good wife, and I hope you have not chosen her when you were drunk. So you have a wife, one you have chosen, the one God dealt you. You realize you are fortunate in your wife. She is enough for you. You have to stick with the hand God has dealt you. We can't all be handsomer, richer, which we might like to be. You must be content, realize when you are happy and not be envious of others.

'So I said to Joe, Joe, you are lucky here. You are happy here. Love oozes out of Wimbledon for you. You are surrounded by excellent, hard-working, honest people. Joe, it is too sad ... I was so upset by what he had told me. It was a bombshell.

'Then I thought, has he been tapped? Has Celtic really offered him a job? In all the years he was with me, there were stories in the papers, yes, but no one ever came to me.

'I felt so emotional. I had to walk around for about three hours, before I had calmed down. Then I had to hurry. No point in dilly-dally. The team's confidence had gone and the caretaker managers were having a hard time.

'I did talk later to Joe about who should take over. We discussed Egil Olsen. I listened to what he had to say.

'But what I can't understand is why Joe led me to believe he had a bigger job lined up. Why, why? I don't understand it ...'

Well, perhaps he thought one would come along, and he didn't want to appear to be leaving for no reason.

'In that case, what an asshole. He could have stayed on, full pay, for as long as he liked. I don't understand it. Why did this bitch of a thing happen? You tell me. When he was so devoted. When we all loved him.'

Yes, you've said that, several times.

'I blame the heart attack. That's what caused all this. It was the heart attack which gave him time to reflect ...'

Part Four

Life After Wimbledon

Chapter Thirty-seven

And so into the new millennium. When 2000 dawned, Joe had by then been unemployed for nine months since his heart attack. He considered he was totally recovered, but no definite managerial job had come his way, not any that he fancied. Meanwhile, the media offers were flooding in.

He was still making his regular trips to Dublin, to pontificate on the English clubs competing in Europe, plus occasional other television work. When I went to see him one morning, he'd just done something for one of the BBC's new channels. 'It was BBC Choice. I hadn't realized I would be commenting on a match with a studio guest – who turned out to be some pop star, who used to be in Take That, or something.

'The show also turned out to be a phone-in, which meant that at vital moments, when Manchester United were about to score, and I'm describing the exciting action, someone would ring in and say "Robbie, your hair is looking lovely this evening, can I ask you where you get your gell?"

'There were also a few calls for me – from old ladies in Donegal asking me when I would be back in work, and whether I would like to have the Irish job. I said I didn't know nothing about any jobs at the moment, but I wanted to be in work soon.'

Joe told the story in his usual way, with lots of guffaws, hamming it up. As we sat and chatted, there was an urgent message on his answerphone, an over-excited voice asking Joe to ring him back as soon as possible.

Joe listened to the message, without picking up the phone. 'It's him again. He's been ringing me all week. He says he's in a consortium to buy a club, and they want me as their manager. Oh yeah, I said, which club? He said it's secret. They've signed an agreement not to talk about it, but it's going to happen. By next Tuesday, it should be all signed and sealed. That was a week ago.

'He asked if I was on the shortlist for anywhere, or had applied for anywhere. I said I don't apply. Everyone in football knows my CV. He says, oh your CV is perfect for us, Joe. Just what we want, a high-profile manager who has performed miracles.

'Aye-aye I thought. He's just like the rest of them, thinking I can do another Wimbledon again, all on a shoestring.

'I asked him how much money he'd got. He wouldn't say at first. I said it's pointless even discussing it, unless you've got money to spend. I've been through all that when I talked to someone at Notts Forest. They wanted me to do it without deep pockets.

'He then says we'll pay you very well as manager. How much is very well? He says £250,000 a year. I said forget it. I was getting that four years ago. He said oh but there would be bonuses and a five-year contract which would be watertight. Whatever happened, you would get your five years paid up, no arguments.

'I said this club you're thinking of buying, it must be a pretty poor club. He said no it's not, but he still can't reveal it. So I say come on, I have to know how much will be available. He says he's got £40 million himself. He's big in the internet, some IT thing, which he's just sold. The names didn't mean a thing to me, but it sounded impressive. All together, he said, he thought his consortium would be able to raise £70 million. So that sounded quite good. But I promised nothing. Just told him to ring me back when he could tell me the whole story. I think he's a dreamer. There are a lot around in football. But some of them do manage to get the money together.'

We discussed which club it might be, the one the internet mogul thought he might be going to buy. We decided it must be either Crystal Palace or Luton.

'He might get Palace for nothing, then have to spend £20 million to pay off their debts. That would leave me £50 million to spend. Luton you'd probably get for £10 million. You'd have to build a new stadium which could be £20 million.

'It's all bollocks, of course. He's probably talking fantasy money. But then the money in football these days is fantasy money. You hear of transfer deals of £30 million or £40 million and you can't believe them – then they come true.'

Chapter Thirty-eight

Watching from afar, as she had been all these years from downtown Watford, was Greta Kinnear, Joe's mother, whom he goes to see fairly regularly. She has been a widow for over 20 years, since the death of her second husband, Gerry Kinnear. But she hasn't lived alone. Her daughter Louise, her first child by Gerry, died from cancer in 1993, aged only 39. Since then, after a court battle, she has been bringing up Louise's two sons, her grandsons. Joe has paid for their education, at a private Catholic college. Today, one is at university and the other is still at home.

Altogether, she has 12 grandchildren, counting of course Joe's two, which they all do in the family.

'It turned out very well for Joseph, him marrying Bonnie. I was a bit shocked, that she was not a Catholic, as I'm from the old school. But they've had 30 years together, in some bad times, when she's hardly seen him, but it has lasted. She has made him very happy. But Bonnie's been lucky as well, oh yes, extremely lucky.'

You mean by marrying such a lovely, nice bloke?

'I didn't just mean that. I mean she's been round the world, since meeting Joe. She's been received in places she would never have got to. She's been received by heads of state in where was it, that Arab place. Oh yes, she's been lucky. I know Joseph will go mad at me saying it, but that's what I think ...'

She's also of course followed his career, not just his marriage, but from afar, as she never went to watch Wimbledon play. But what caused her great grief was football fans and newspaper people going on about one particular aspect of Joe's life.

'You have to put up with it, when you are in the public eye, but some of the things said about Joe were terrible. I remember every one. I don't forget. Horrible things, said not about Bonnie's husband – but my son! I was furious.

'Oh you know, making remarks about his big belly, shouting abuse about him being fat. We might say it in the family, but if outsiders say it, then I go mad. I want to wallop them. Those guys shouting it, or writing it in the papers. They just want to look in the mirror more often. I know who they were. I've remembered their names.'

But did you actually say to Joe himself that he was perhaps putting on a bit too much weight?

'Of course I did. I'd say look after your health son, that's what matters most. He'd say I'm okay mum, stop worrying.

'But I could see he was self-destroying. Travelling all those thousands of miles each week, filling himself up with fish and chips every night. He was hardly ever at home. Bonnie missed the prime years with him.

'Then I worried about his throat. He always had problems with his swallowing. It's how he was born. Doing all that screaming and shouting, that didn't help.

'I don't think he got the credit he deserved for all those years at Wimbledon, struggling to keep them in the top division. Could any of those managers at Man. Utd, or Arsenal or Chelsea, with all their money, could they have done what Joseph did?

'The day of his heart attack, I didn't expect it, not that day, but I knew he was killing himself. Young Das, my grandson, was at home doing his homework on the table there. He had some radio station on and they gave a newsflash. He didn't quite catch it, but he thought he heard the name Joe Kinnear. He told me and I said it must be something about the team, getting beaten or something.

'Then there was another flash, about Joe himself. Something had happened to him. So I put the telly on – and they said Joe

Kinnear had had a heart attack. I was in a state of shock. I just sat there in the chair, unable to get out of it.

'Then the phone rang and it was Bonnie. Had I heard the news, she said. I said yes, but didn't know anything. She said she didn't know much either. She was going to go up to Sheffield. I hadn't to worry. She'd keep me informed.

'She rang when she'd been to see him. I wanted to go up, but she said no, he needed total peace and rest. But our Carmen went up. I did what I was told. He didn't want any more pressures.

'When I eventually saw him, I was shocked. He'd had a tap on the shoulder. Next time he might not be so lucky.

'Now he's better, I hope he won't go back to a Wimbledon sort of job again, digging a hole for himself. Nothing is worth that. Personally I'd like him to be manager of Ireland. I don't think that would be too stressful. But he tells me he wants to get back to a big club.'

So what about Bonnie, what did she think about Joe and his future?

'I don't want him to go back to a Wimbledon situation. But of course the clubs who will be after him will want him to do another Wimbledon. That's what he's been famous for. Keeping a club at the top on a low budget. I'd prefer if he was at a lower club, with lower expectations, where things can just tick over.

'I left the Wimbledon decision to him. But it seemed to me it wasn't really football to blame for what happened – but his lifestyle. That was what had to change. He has changed his personal lifestyle, but once he finds another job in football, his working life will be much the same. I'll probably never see him again. But, you learn the hard way how to survive.'

Any tips you could pass on?

'My advice to any woman thinking of marrying a footballer? Don't. No, that's a joke. You just have to realize that you are not marrying the man you are marrying his career. Anyone who is successful in football has to be totally committed. There is no other way, for player or manager.

'Most successful people, in all walks of life, are a bit strange, a bit potty. I've met quite a few. I never know whether they were like that before they started, and that's what helped make them successful, or they become strange with success. Look at Sam. He is so clever, so brilliant at business, but at the same time, well, he's not exactly a normal person.

'Looking back over the 30 years with Joe, I don't regret anything. I'm now looking forward to seeing what's round the corner ...'

Chapter Thirty-nine

One thing Joe wasn't worrying about, while sitting round all those months, waiting for the next thing in his life to come along, was money. There was the Wimbledon pay-off for a start.

'I've never been bothered about earning big money. People always asked me, while I was at Wimbledon, why I had stayed there so long, not gone somewhere bigger. As long as my family are healthy and happy, I'm happy. I can't be bothered with the responsibility of money and possessions. I don't have a second home. I drive an ordinary Rover. I've got simple tastes. And I have been sensible over the last 20 years and saved wisely. I realized early on that there are happy people in Brixton and miserable people in Belgravia. Money can't buy you peace of mind.

'As a manager, I never had any backhanders. Sam looked after all the money anyway, not me. Mind you, agents will often say when they ring you up about a deal "and there will be something in it for you". I never asked what that meant, but it's common-place. And we know it has happened in the past. But I would say it doesn't happen now. Managers are too well paid. I would be surprised if any Premiership manager was taking bungs, after what happened to George Graham. It would be a stupid thing to do, for your career, having an agent with something over you.

'I went into football for the love of it. And it's been a wonderful way to make a living, working outside in the fresh air every day ...'

You are not beginning to think this is the end, a time to look back rather than look forward? Not at your age, and now fully recovered?

'Yeah, but it does make you think. I was speaking to Dave Mackay yesterday. He's coming down to stay with us for a day, while we do the FA Cup draw together. On the phone, he was saying that he and his wife have just been to pick up their pension. He said it was great, getting your pension. They spent it on a good meal, some nice wine, did a bit of shopping, and that was the pension gone.

'Dave Mackay! Collecting his pension! I couldn't believe it. It doesn't sound real, does it? In my mind, he's still Braveheart, the Lion of Spurs, one of the greatest players of all time. Did you notice that George Graham the other day was saying that Dave is his all-time favourite player. He can't be a pensioner, not Dave.'

Dave was born 14 November 1934, in Edinburgh, so he's well and truly over the pensionable age for men.

'I won't be collecting mine for a long time. I reckon I have at least a good 10 years left. But funnily enough, I'm already a "legend" myself. Tonight, we're going to the HMV sports awards in Park Lane. I'm on the top table for legends in football, along with Brian Clough, Alan Mullery, Peter Shilton, Mick Channon, Alex Stepney and Dave. The last one I went to like this, there was an auction and somebody paid £10,000 for a signed photo of Stanley Matthews. Proceeds to charity of course.'

I asked if he was perhaps getting a bit depressed, with nothing much happening.

'Not at all. I've enjoyed the rest. I've now got all my confidence back. I'm fitter than ever.'

But none of the recent vacancies, for which most newspapers tipped you over the last few months, ever came to anything, not even an interview.

'Ah but if you think about it, most of them didn't actually appoint anyone else. It was the papers saying I was on the list if Villa sacked John Gregory, not me. There hasn't actually been a change of manager in the Premiership so far this season, well apart from Hoddle going to Southampton. And that's an unusual case, which I don't quite understand. I do feel very sorry for David Jones. I always found him to be a good guy. But I still get mentioned all the time, if changes are being considered.

'When I *was* depressed, that was lying in the hospital in Sheffield, thinking I'd had it. All I wanted then was to wake up the next day. I didn't think about football. Just the bleep-bleeps. One night it did stop and I was terrified. The noise had changed to a burring sound. I thought that's it. But all I'd done was pull a loose wire out in my sleep, when turning over. The night nurse rushed to put it back in.

'When I was getting better, I'd walk round and talk to the other heart attack victims. Sit on their beds and have a bit of a chit-chat. Most of them were Sheffield Wednesday supporters, so they would try to wind me up, saying Wednesday would finish higher in the league than Wimbledon. That sort of chat. One or two said I would be mad if I ever went back to football again, after what had happened.

'But one bloke suddenly said to me – "How would you like to be remembered Joe?" It was such a strange question. I'd never been asked it before. I didn't know how to answer. The thought had never crossed my mind, till then.'

So how would you answer it now?

'Oh I still don't know. That I was a nice bloke, I suppose. As for football, I'd like to be seen as a good footballer and a good manager ...

'I was thinking the other day I could be an agent. Most agents are hated by managers, and chairmen. No one trusts them. I don't think I've heard of an ex-manager who's become an agent, so it might work well. Agents don't know about football. They don't discover players.

'I'd go scouting, all over the world, sign young players up, then I'd contact managers direct. I'd know who was looking for a striker or whatever. I'd get right through to them, as I know them. I'm a credible person, known as a good judge of players, someone they could trust. Someone like say David Dein at

Arsenal would trust me on a deal. There would be no hidden middle-men. I like to think my name is clean.

'Anyway, it's only an idea. Sitting round thinking, it just came into my head. But nah, I won't do any of that. All I want to be is a manager again ...'

All the same, that thought had come into his head. After almost a year since his heart attack, with no decent job in football being offered, was he subconsciously beginning to think it might be time to bow out? Especially when the Blackburn job was eventually filled – by Graeme Souness, who had much more serious heart trouble than Joe, necessitating a major operation, something that Joe had not needed.

Chapter Forty

I went to see Sam Hammam at his London townhouse near Regents Park – tasteful, artistic, but not overtly luxurious considering the style in which many of today's millionaire players and millionaire chairmen live. He had been up that morning since 5.30, working on his own on a problem. No, nothing to do with Wimbledon. A mathematical problem, for his own amusement, a purely intellectual test, to see if he could crack it. He thought he now saw the solution.

His hair is pure white, and no wonder after 24 years keeping Wimbledon alive and buoyant, but his eyebrows are still strangely dark. He is aged 53, same age as Joe, but looks fitter, healthier, sharp and agile. When I said as much he said that in fact he and Joe are on the same pills. He takes his to control his cholesterol level.

I suppose he, like Joe, must have got pretty fed up with all the struggles over the years, working so hard, just to keep them where they are, but he wouldn't admit it. He did say that one day he will return to Lebanon, his native land, where he still has a house.

His charming, self-effacing, dignified wife, Nada, served us Turkish coffee, which Sam instructed her to make properly, not to weaken it, the way she often did for English guests. She also brought a bowl of freshly peeled oranges and a glass of water for each of us. An hour later, she appeared with a bowl of delicious small tomatoes, plus more glasses of water.

214

Sam had got over the shock of Joe leaving, if only just, and professed himself to be pleased with the progress that the new manager, Egil Olsen, was then making.

'I now have to accept our love affair with Joe is at an end. But I love him still and will try my best to help him personally. That is my aim now, to get Joe a good job. All he knows is football. What else can he do?

'If he gets another job, it will be 70 per cent me and 30 per cent him. Of course it will. Any chairman interested in Joe will ring me and say tell me the truth, what is Joe like? And I will tell him the truth, that Joe is very very good. I want Joe to get a good job.

'But I have been clever. When I've heard a job might he coming up, and their chairman has not rung me, I haven't rung him. They would suspect something, that I am trying to get rid of Joe. What I've done is ring Joe's agent. I've said ring so and so chairman, say you've heard there might be a job going, say Joe is available, why not ring Sam Hammam, get it from the horse's mouth?

'But we are still waiting. I hope he will get something. And a good one. If he goes to a small club, with a smaller crowd, I'll start thinking again, why why why why, why did you leave Wimbledon?

'Whether he can succeed with £20 million or £40 million to spend, who knows. He's never done it. So you don't know, till he does. The whole thing is a tragedy. I am beginning to feel emotional again, just thinking about ...'

I let him pause, while we refreshed ourselves with a good healthy glass of water and a small tomato. Would you have Joe back at Wimbledon? If say Olsen didn't hack it, or went back to Norway, and Joe is still available? Would you offer him the job? Stranger things have happened in football. Sam thought for a while.

'Joe needs to get this out of his system. Some time has to burn. No manager has ever come back to Wimbledon. I don't know. I don't know. I miss him being around. But, life moves on.

'My aim now is to get him the best job I can. I love him. We will be buddy-buddies for ever ...'

Chapter Forty-one

Joe's own best buddies, during his Wimbledon years, would seem to have been the players. Not one of them, even those who have moved on, have a bad word to say about him. Those who were still there, like Robbie Earle, missed him every day.

'It's a different sort of spirit now,' said Robbie. 'The antics still go on, but we have a quieter set of players. We haven't got the characters like Vinnie and Fash any more. Joe encouraged the Crazy Gang image and played up to it. He'd often whisper in your ear that he didn't like so and so's new trousers, and that would be a sign for the lads to do something. He believed the camaraderie we felt for each other off the pitch would carry over on to the pitch, which it did. When playing Manchester United we never felt overawed or overrun.'

Robbie came from Port Vale in 1990, to be met by the usual initiation rite. 'I had been warned, but didn't really know what to expect, as this was my first big club. I was told not to fight it, and they'll only do it once. Nothing happened in the dressing room, then we were sent off on a mile-long run to Wimbledon Common to warm up. When we got there, they jumped on me, took off all my clothes. I had to run back to the training ground, in public, absolutely naked. All they gave me was a traffic cone to cover my embarrassment.'

His first impression of Joe was that he was very different from any other coach he had met. 'He struck me as bolshie, alien to the sort of doing-it-by-the-book coaches. Joe didn't

217

bother much with paperwork. He did seem a larger-than-life figure. We were all very pleased when he got the manager's job. We were asked our opinion and we were unanimous in wanting him.

'One of the early incidents he had to deal with was a fight at the training ground between Fash and Laurie Sanchez. They were two very strong characters. Undercurrents had been simmering for some time, then came to a head when they physically started fighting. I was one of those who pulled them apart. I think Joe fined them, made them apologize, but he settled it so well, and internally. The story never came out.

'He did have a sensible touch when it came to discipline. We were once abroad, and given a curfew of 11 o'clock, but 10 of us decided to sneak out of our hotel and have a drink. We got to this bar, and were all having a beer, when we saw Joe and Terry Burton arriving at the front door. We all dived behind the bar and one by one we crawled across the floor and out of a side door. Then we went like hell back to the hotel. We were all pleased, thinking we'd got away with it and not been spotted. But next morning, at training, Joe said I want to see you 10, after training. We all got a little fine and a telling off, but that was all. Nothing drastic, and no one else ever knew.

'He was always open to discussion, and would listen to our ideas. Often he would make it look as if we were playing the way we wanted to play, that a system had been our idea, which was good psychology. If it failed, then we couldn't blame him. But he was also very quick to change systems and is tactically brilliant. At first when he changed things, like moving five up front when we were already one goal down, I'd think how stupid, we'll lose now, but it happened so many times that his changes worked. I realized it wasn't luck but skill.

'I suppose the only minor criticism I'd have is that he didn't always tell people to their face how good they were, how much he rated them. He'd tell me, or others, but not them. Perhaps he thought they'd get too cocky, or lose respect for him.

'Joe always made you feel that he felt what you felt. In victory or defeat, he would react as we did. And he'd be as physically drained as we were.

'He managed by his emotions. In his team-talks, you could tell he felt everything. Egil Olsen is more studious. Joe would rant and rave when things went wrong. That's not Egil's way. He doesn't trade in emotions. He has everything on the computer.

'After working under Joe for nine years, I was used to him and his methods, and saw them succeeding. What of course you don't know is whether the manager changes you, and your personality.

'On the day of his heart attack, something strange happened. About 1.30, while we were in the hotel in Sheffield, he called me to his room, saying come and have a chat. We often did that, for 10 minutes or so before a game. This time I was with him for two whole hours. I'd never been with him as long, or heard him talk so openly. Not just about the game ahead, but about Wimbledon, how he loved all the players, how much they meant to him, how he loved working with us, how happy he had been. It struck me at the time as weird. I didn't know what it meant.

'Then when he had the heart attack, I thought that's it, he'd had a premonition, perhaps without knowing it. That was why he had talked so openly – as if he might be leaving us ...

'In that chat, he did go over the terrible disappointment of our recent defeat in the Cup by Spurs. That still preyed on his mind. He was naturally emotional, but I think after those three failed semis, the stress was getting to him more. He so wanted to win something, to prove himself as a manager.

'I hope he does go back to football, for his sake. If it's in you, it's in you. Joe is not the sort of person to go golfing or sit around at home. If he doesn't go back, it will be football's loss. There aren't many like Joe. I didn't just look upon him as a manager, and I'd say he was the best man-manager I've ever met. I classed him as a friend.'

Perhaps Joe's closest friend amongst the players was Vinnie Jones, now the well-known thespian. As we have seen, they still go out together to social occasions, despite the fact that Joe is 20 years older and from a different generation.

'I was watching that Sheffield Wednesday match at home,' says Vinnie, 'when Joe had his heart attack. I rang Bonnie and said I'll drive you up, this moment if you want, but she didn't.

'I saw Joe as soon as he came home again. I just couldn't believe the thousands of cards he had from well-wishers. I knew he was well liked, but not that much. I laughed and joked with him, tried to cheer him. I said I never knew he had a heart, so how comes he had a heart attack. When he started getting better, I organized days out for him, either to the dogs or racing.

'Of all the managers I had in my career, Joe was the only one who treated players like an equal. He had trust in you. In training he'd go on at you about being overweight, or drinking too much or whatever, but he wasn't the sort of manager who rings your house at 10 o'clock on Friday evening to check you're at home.

'I didn't really want to return to Wimbledon in 1992, but Chelsea made it clear it was my best option, financially. So I met Sam and Joe at the Watford Hilton and eventually agreed. I did ask to be captain, and Joe agreed straight away.

'I had never met him before, but I knew he was from Watford. By a coincidence, my mother had once worked at the Watford pub Joe took over, when she was learning to run a pub herself.

'Because I'd been at Wimbledon before, I was too cute for them on my first day at training. I turned up in shorts and flip-flops. So they didn't manage to get me.

'It did a lot for me and my career, Joe making me captain. We had a proper captain-manager relationship and it brought out the best in me. Now and again I would go out drinking with him, have a few beers on our day off, go to the races, then next day at training he would have a right go at me, say I'd been drinking too much. I thought bugger this, I'm not going out with him again, if he's going to hold it against me.

'He did have problems motivating people like Marcus Gayle. Gayley would collapse after 20 minutes of a game, as if he'd had a puncture. Joe would go spare, screaming and swearing at him.

Little Joe, ranting at this six-foot-three black feller, who was so strong, so quick. Joe really would go mental – because he cared so much, he knew how good Gayley could be. But it was having the wrong effect on him. Joe's methods were not working. If Marcus had been a boozer, then Joe would have been more on his wavelength, understood him, but Marcus is not like that. He's a churchgoer.

'So eventually I told Joe, let me handle this, I'll get Marcus going, you leave off him for a while. And it worked. Then Joe changed tactics and said to Marcus I'm going to play you for the next 10 games, whether you play rubbish or not. That was what changed it for Marcus, being given Joe's confidence.

'In training, if we had some ideas, he would let us try them out. Usually they didn't work and he'd say that was rubbish, now we'll do it my way. There was one time he brought in a young reserve and I said Joe, you can't put him in, he'll get eaten alive, he won't survive, he'll be out of his depth. But Joe brought him in purely to do a marking job. It totally worked, leaving the rest of us to get on with our game.

'Joe did take part in a lot of the Crazy Gang stuff. And he encouraged us to do things like letting down people's tyres. But a lot of the things we did were kept in house. There was a sort of code of practice that we didn't reveal in print certain personal things about each other. Just the funny things.

'I remember in Sweden once on some close-season tour we were playing this little local club, amateurs I think, most of them farmers, and they beat us 1-0. Joe went ape. He gave us such a bollocking and then he said that's it, none of yous are coming to the reception tonight, none of you will have a drink, you'll all stay in your hotel, all evening.

'I told the lads don't worry, I'll fix it. I got them all in their training kit and went to the restaurant near the harbour, where the reception was being held. Joe was inside, having a drink with their manager and officials.

'We then ran up and down like hell outside the window, back and forward, doing press-ups, everything. Till at last Joe came out. His face lit up in this big Irish smile. "Okay lads," he said, "you can come in and have a beer ..."

'I think he has fully recovered now. No doubt about that. It's the old Joe again, fit and raring to go. He could earn as much money in the media as he could in football. I've told him all that. He's a natural on television. But I can sense that deep down he wants to manage a big club. In a way I suppose he hasn't fulfilled his career, till he does so.

'And I'm sure he will. He has such respect from everyone in football. Every time I go out with him, and we meet other football people, other managers, they all admire him so much.

'I'd say he was the most honest manager I've ever worked with. He made training fun, allowed you to enjoy yourself, but once the real work started, he was very hard. What I liked best about him as a manager was that he treated you like a man.'

Chapter Forty-two

Joe was much more cheerful when I saw him next. His phone hadn't stopped ringing, not that he was answering most of the calls. It meant that 30 messages had piled up on his answerphone, most concerning job offers, engagements or ideas.

'I'm suddenly getting internet people offering me fortunes to put my name to football pages on the web sites, whatever that means. Just had one from Finland that sounds interesting. There's so much money out there, now that football is so fashionable. I could have a very easy, well-paid life, just talking about football.'

One of the engagements he had agreed to was an appearance in a hotel in Jersey along with Vinnie Jones, being interviewed by a well-known TV football presenter.

'It's a private thing, some big international firm getting all its top executives together for a conference. Me and Vinnie are the sort of entertainment, the after-dinner cabaret. I get a free weekend, big dinner, and I only have to talk for 15 minutes and I get three grand. Can't be bad.

'I've had about 20 invites to make after-dinner speeches in the last few weeks, for good money – yet I've never done one in my life.

'The Jersey trip should be fun with Jonah. He's always a laugh, though he's on a health kick, as he has to be fit to be an actor. He's threatening to ring the papers, tell them I'm going to Jersey – and I'm going to meet Jack Walker. You know, the owner of Blackburn. He says that should make a page in the *Sun*, and really stir things up ...'

Two other new possibilities had recently arisen. One of them was at Celtic where John Barnes had lost his job. Joe had received a call from a Scottish Deep Throat, saying he was ringing on behalf of some Celtic directors, wanting to meet Joe.

'I don't know who he is, how genuine it is. Football is full of middle-men, some of them chancers and conmen. This bloke did seem well connected. I said if they wanted me to come and talk to them, I would.

'Then my agent has been talking to someone called Max Clifford. Never heard of him. Who is he?'

I explained that Mr Clifford is a well-known public relations man, known for selling kiss-and-tell celebrity stories to the tabloids. He had recently become a sort of PR man for Fulham Football Club and Mr Fayed, the owner.

'Yeah, he did mention Fulham. He wants my agent to have lunch with him. Nothing to lose. See what he has to offer.'

In the year since his heart attack, there had been lots of phone calls, several meetings, but only two producing what could be called serious offers. One was from Oxford United. He wasn't really interested, but met their representatives at a hotel at King's Cross, before saying no. The other a more high profile club which had asked him not to reveal their name.

'I had about five hours with their people. They wanted me to bring them back up to the Premiership, but without spending any real money. They said ah, but with your proven record, you can make us good without spending millions.

'I am going to be very choosy about what I do next. I'm not going to take anything, just for the sake of being in work. When I left Wimbledon, which was because of the heart attack, I wanted a complete rest from football. Some may have thought I had another job lined up, but I hadn't. I just wanted to take stock. Sam would never believe me.'

Would you take the Ireland job, if it came up?

'I was interviewed on many occasions by Louis Kilcoyne and

the board of the Irish FA about the possibility of me being the next Ireland manager after Jack Charlton. I knew Lewis was very keen to give me the job. He was the President of the FA at the time. On my second visit, I took Sam along with me. He drove us to the London Airport Hotel. After talking things over with the Irish FA I told them I would be proud to be manager of Ireland one day, but at that time I still felt I had a job to do at Wimbledon in the Premiership. I didn't think the timing was right. I still wanted to be playing the Manchester Uniteds, Arsenals, Chelseas, Liverpools and Spurs, having big games every week. It was the hardest decision I ever had to make.'

Do you regret now not taking it?

'At the time I didn't. But if it came up again now, I would be interested. It's probably a better time for me to do it now, but of course these things never come up when you want them.

'I loved my time playing for Ireland, and I'm very proud of all my 26 caps. From my debut game in 1967 to my last game in 1976 against Switzerland, when we played at home, I always went to my grandmother's house in Kimmage in Dublin. The day before, when we'd finished training, I'd pop round and she would light the fire and make me a cup of tea and a slice of brack – that's a famous Dublin cake. She's fill me in on all the gossip about any of my old school pals who still lived in the local streets. After the match, I'd come back and see her, before flying back to Tottenham. If we'd got beat, she used to give me a right earbashing. "What sort of performance was that? You must have been out drinking all night." I'd reply that we probably would have played better, if we had been out drinking.

'I played with some very good professionals – and had to deal with some crusty old directors. Two players I consider great were Johnny Giles and Paul McGrath. I had some good crack with Eamonn Dunphy. He was my roommate, when we played for Ireland, and used to make me a good cup of tea in the morning. But I have to say we didn't really have all that many great players, in my 10 years playing for my country. There were a few who played like elephants in hobnailed boots.

'The third great Irish player is one still playing today – Roy Keane. He's the star man, the heart of the team, for his club and country. If he's getting £50,000 a week, as reported, then he's worth it. If I was Manchester United manager, I'd pay it, and so would any other manager. I don't believe his team-mates were demanding the same as him. I bet they were just delighted he stayed. I doubt if Manchester United would have had such success without him. Would you expect Odd Job in a James Bond movie to get paid the same as Sean Connery? Of course not.

'I would like the opportunity again to manage the national side, but I might have blown it. I don't think FAI [the Irish FA] were very pleased with me over the Wimbledon-Dublin fiasco. This was an absolutely genuine plan. With Wimbledon not having our own ground, we'd tried so many ways, for so long, to give ourselves a base, create our own home. The idea was we'd move the club to Dublin, but stay in the English Premier League.

'I was all for it. So was Sam. We had the ground lined up and all the funding. I wanted to call ourselves Dublin United. We'd have the biggest stadium in Ireland, the biggest support, and become not just the biggest club in Ireland, but in all Europe. I'm not kidding. By being in the Premiership, with all that support and TV money, we'd be in Europe most seasons, playing Juventus and Barcelona. Think what that would have done for Irish football. We could become the new Holland.

'We wouldn't lose talented young Irish boys to the English or Scottish clubs. We'd have our own school of excellence. Football fans would go around Dublin wearing Dublin United shirts, not Manchester United or Celtic. It would give kids in the backstreets hope and inspiration. They would see with their own eyes what was possible, which they can't imagine at present.

'But it all failed. The Irish FA said it would ruin Ireland's own national league, which I don't believe. The English First Division survives, despite being in the shadow of the Premiership. So that was a shame. But they might come back, if the national job comes up.

'It's sad in a way that you get a job as a football manager because someone has had the sack. That's how it works. My next job will be someone's pain. So these last six months it's been an uncomfortable feeling, waiting for someone to lose his job. I wouldn't wish that on anyone. Far better when a manager leaves of his own free will, to go on to something better, like Kevin Keegan leaving Fulham for England. Now if George Graham had to leave Spurs for Barcelona, and they offered me the job, that would be fantasy all round ...'

If nothing decent does come up, will you be disappointed?

'Yes, very. After all, Bobby Robson is still managing a top team at 67. I'm only 53 and feel very fit. I have the same chances as anyone else now, the doctors have told me that.

'In fact I'm better off than I was before. The doctors said that as well. The shock has helped me. I know about my heart, which I didn't know before. I know how to treat it properly this time.

'I was stupid in the past. Bonnie would book an annual medical check for me, then I'd cancel it at the last minute. I'd ring and lie and say we were going on holiday. I just couldn't be bothered. I won't be silly like that again. I now look after myself properly. Bonnie's right. What would I do without her ...'

Chapter Forty-three

It was almost exactly a year to the day, at the end of February 2000, that Joe decided to go back to Wimbledon. His first appearance there since his heart attack, despite repeated invitations. 'I haven't wanted to put pressure on the new manager, get in his hair. I knew the fans would shout my name out if I went there, so I thought I'd stay away.'

It happened to be a home game against Manchester United, the big game, the glamour game of every season, with a full house. Joe was looking forward to seeing his friend Fergie again. Sir Alex Ferguson, a great admirer of what Joe had done at Wimbledon, had been one of the first to contact him after his heart attack. On his recovery, he had invited him for a day's racing, to watch his own horse race at Ascot and join him in a private box.

It also turned out to be an important day for Wimbledon Football Club. To the surprise of the football world, Sam Hammam had announced that he was selling his remaining shares, finally giving up control of his beloved club. Since the arrival of the Norwegians he had still been in day-to-day control, but the relationship with one of them had deteriorated. That now appeared to be the end of Sam and the Crazy Gang.

On the day before, during a training session, he had told the Wimbledon players what he was going to do and naturally, they gave him a send-off, in true Wimbledon style. Despite the fact that he was in a good suit, they had grabbed him, thrown him up in the air, then chucked him in a pool of water.

All the newspapers, TV and radio were saying it was the end of an era. A year ago, Joe had gone, their longest serving manager. Now it was farewell to Sam the man. Vinnie Jones was quoted in the *Sun* as saying he would no longer be interested in Wimbledon. 'I'll look for their results, but I won't get the same arse ache when they lose.' Being the *Sun*, a newspaper noted for its decorum and decency, they didn't print such a rude word. What Vinnie was quoted as saying was '**** ache'. I suppose it could have been 'head ache'.

Joe and Bonnie left their Mill Hill home at mid-morning on the Saturday in a mini-cab, heading across London towards the Crystal Palace ground, a journey which Joe had done many times. It appeared to be a first time for the driver, a foreign gentleman, so Bonnie sat in front and directed him through strange places like Trafalgar Square and Whitehall and then across the river.

I sat in the back with Joe. Must be so nice, I said, going to see Wimbledon play without being all churned up inside, worrying about the things that could go wrong. Not really, he said: he'd rather be going to a match as a manager rather than a spectator.

But surely it will be a pleasant change not spending 90 minutes screaming and shouting and not needing 24 hours to get your voice back afterwards. Not of course that you'll do that again, not after what you've been through. You'll change your ways, next time around.

'No, not really.'

But you won't be doing all that scouting, rushing round the country, tearing back along the motorways in the early hours?

'Oh yeah, still do that.'

But Joe, that was part of the stress. You have to sub-let some of the scouting in the lower leagues. Or watch more videos.

'Oh, I've got to see them. A manager can't sign anyone he hasn't watched personally for a decent number of games.'

Coaching then – no need to be on the training pitch every day and all day. Let some other coaches take charge.

'You can't. You have to be there. Ordinary coaches can have

trouble with a stroppy player, someone who gives lip, refuses to do something. That can upset the whole training.

'Certain players will do it, knowing the coach can't really discipline them. If they try it on me, they've had it. They're back in the reserves or on their arse, out of the club.

'And let's say we've had a bad result, got stuffed 5-0. On the Monday morning, I need to be on at them from the first minute, put the fear of death into them all week, so that the performance is not repeated. Only a manager can do that.

'So you see, I can't give up taking training. Next time I might take the odd walk round the pitches and just watch, but that's about all.'

Okay then, but no doubt you'll lessen the hours next time, making sure you're home to Bonnie several nights a week by seven o'clock?

'No, can't do that either.'

Bonnie had been listening, while directing the driver. She made a face at me in the mirror. 'Keep trying,' she said, 'but you won't get anywhere. I've tried all that.'

But Joe, I said, all managers, all bosses, do their job better if they take breaks and delegate some of their work.

'That's just it,' said Bonnie, 'he can't delegate.'

I could see Joe was getting fed up with me going on at him, so we moved on to discussing Sam. Joe knew only what he'd read that morning but couldn't believe Sam would just walk away from football. Perhaps he had a plan to buy Crystal Palace or join another club.

He then started telling Sam stories, about him making dopey bets with the players when they were travelling.

'He'd play them at cards for money, and lose, paying them hundreds in cash, but he'd usually win at Trivial Pursuits. Then he'd say double or quits and keep doing it till the player won.

'In training he'd bet Sully [goalkeeper Neil Sullivan] £20 a time that he could score a penalty against him. He'd run up and kick the ball like a three year old. He had no chance ever of scoring. But he seemed to love paying out the bets.

'Then he'd challenge players to a race the length of the pitch – £50 if you could beat him. The only condition was that he could start at the halfway line. Everyone could still beat him, but they'd slow down as they overtook him.

'When I signed Dean Holdsworth, I told Sam what a great goalscorer he was, how well he would do for us. So at the beginning of his first full season, Sam bet him he wouldn't score more than 20 goals in the season. If Deano did better than that, he got some huge sum of money, I've forgotten what, but Sam also promised to kiss his arse.

'Well before the season ended, Deano had beaten that, and got 24 goals in all that season (1993-94). So he had won his bet. Sam had to kiss his arse in public, that was part of the bet. That meant at the training ground, in front of all the lads. That morning all of them were saying to Deano, "Make sure you have a shit beforehand." Sam did it. Dean dropped his shorts and Sam did kiss his arse.'

Yes, it's hard to imagine another chairman of a Premier League club acting quite as Sam Hammam had done.

'He was just as Crazy as the rest of us. Our chairman was a great character as well, Stanley Reed, a 90-year-old eccentric. I hear he's ill so I'm going to visit him next week. One of my abiding memories of my years at Wimbledon will be old Stanley leading the singing.

'After every match, in all the 10 years I was there, win or lose, Stanley would come into our dressing room afterwards and get us singing. Naturally we didn't feel like singing if we'd just got stuffed, but he did it all the same. If we'd won, then the atmosphere was electric.

'He always led us in the same song. "Come on you lot," he'd say, "are you ready?" Then he'd start us all off:

> Here we are again,
> Happy as can be,
> All good pals and jolly good company.
> Never mind the weather

Never mind the rain,
Here we are together
Whoops, we're at it again.
La di da dee
La di da de da,
All good pals and jolly good company."

'I remember him once doing it in Norway when we were on a pre-season tour and had just played Molde. We had this reception, with their club, players and officials. After the speeches, Stanley made all the team get up on stage and he led them in our legendary song. It was weird. There he was, conducting all these young players – as if Boyzone had got themselves a 90-year-old lead singer. Ah, happy memories.'

We got to the ground at one o'clock, two hours before kick-off, but there were already lots of coaches and crowds there, mainly Manchester United supporters. They of course tend not to live in Manchester, but are here there and everywhere.

Joe told the driver to drive straight in, ignore any notices. He was immediately recognized by several officials. When we got out of the car, some fans rushed over, wanting his autograph. A father asked if his son could stand beside Joe for a photograph. Everyone wanted to know if Joe was coming back to the club.

Sam had left three tickets for us for the directors' box and the boardroom, which was kind. Bonnie and I went straight up but Joe went off to look for Fergie. In his management days, he always had a glass of red wine with Fergie before each game.

In the boardroom were the Manchester United directors, the Wimbledon directors, guests and friends. I was ticked off by one Wimbledon director for not wearing a tie, which I never do, nor a suit. But I thought I was quite smart, for me. Later when I looked at my invite to the directors' box, before filing it with my football memorabilia, I noticed that it said 'no jeans or trainers'. They do have standards, these football directors.

By chance that day, there was another ex-Wimbledon manager present, Bobby Gould, in charge from 1987-90. I told him how Sam had said how upset he was when Bobby had left the club, saying he was a rolling stone, who liked moving on.

'Bollocks,' said Bobby. 'It was money. I wanted £60,000 a year. Sam was offering me £50,000. But I did love my time there and I loved Sam. Still do.' Oh, so much love around in football, who would have believed it.

Everyone was very friendly and hospitable and the food and wine were excellent, served buffet style from a large table in the middle of the room with a generous supply of hot and cold dishes. I found myself standing beside Sir Roland Smith, chairman of Manchester United PLC. I asked him how Wimbledon hospitality compared with other Premiership boardrooms. He said he always liked coming here, but couldn't say which was the best. 'Bobby Charlton keeps a list and gives them scores.'

I then talked to some other directors, and their wives, and one told me they thought Spurs was about the least welcoming. Their directors tend to sit in cliques. At Wimbledon, people were moving around, introducing each other, though I did notice a party of Norwegians who seemed to stick together, sticking to their own language. There was also an ambassador present, but I didn't find out which country he was from.

Alex Ferguson appeared and all heads turned to stare. He said hello to a few people, then sat down with Alastair Campbell, Tony Blair's chief press spokesman, whom I had not noticed till then, though he is a friend and neighbour of mine. They were soon deep in whispered conversation.

When Fergie had gone, I asked Alastair what plots they had been hatching, but he wouldn't tell me. Fergie is a known Labour supporter, which may not always endear him to some of the more right-wing Man. Utd directors. And Alastair is a Burnley fan, so what was he doing here? One of his sons is a mad Man. Utd fan, that was the reason, but Alastair was wearing his Burnley scarf.

Joe appeared just before kick-off. He'd been with Fergie, and talked to some of the Man. Utd players, then been to the Wimbledon dressing room door and talked to some of them.

'Alan Kimble said to me "Am I in gaffer?" and I said, yes you're in the team as Ben Thatcher's injured. There were lots of remarks like that. John Hartson has invited me to his wedding in the summer. I've already been to the christening of his child.

'Egil Olsen came up and said he now knows what a hard job I had to do here. He was very friendly. I wished them all the best of luck in the game.'

I sat with Joe in the directors' box during the match, which was most enlightening. Wimbledon started brilliantly, Jason Euell scored after a minute, but slowly Man. Utd began to get a grip. Joe pointed out that Carl Cort was playing out of position, in midfield as opposed to up front as a central striker which he prefers. 'Look, you'll see his head dropping when he has to get up and down all the time.'

At free kicks and corners, Joe explained what the team plan had been, and who should have been doing what. In a way I hoped Joe didn't get another job, so I can go to games with him and he can explain things I miss.

Under Olsen, Wimbledon's defence had changed to zonal marking. With Joe, they marked man to man. 'If you have world-class players, clever and skilful, then zonal marking is fine, but otherwise it's best to mark man to man. Everyone then knows what they are supposed to do.'

And of course get given a bollocking, if they don't do it, and Joe happens to be their manager.

'You have to keep on at them. All week you practise certain corners, then come the day, someone will take a quick short corner, and give the ball away. I'll say at half time, what the fuck did you do that for? None of the defence had time to come up, take the positions we had planned. He'll mutter something about it seeming like a good idea at the time. Oh, you have to keep at them. No use sitting quietly in the stand, making notes. Not for me anyway. Someone has to be there to change things.'

During the match, while I was trying to listen to Joe's inside observations, Alastair Campbell was in front of me, muttering into his mobile or his pager. Must be ringing the prime minister,

234

I thought, arranging to hang out someone's dirty washing – I wish he'd stop it, so annoying. I found out later he'd been ringing a friend at Burnley's match who had promised to ring him with any scores but hadn't got through.

The Wimbledon game finished 2-2, which was fair on chances, though Man. Utd had most of the possession and were pressing very hard towards the end. A good result for Wimbledon and the Premier League, as it stopped Man. Utd getting too far ahead.

Afterwards in the boardroom, there were more drinks and sandwiches while people crowded round the TV set to see the other scores.

Alastair's children were thrilled because Sam had taken them to see the players in the tunnel before kick-off. David Beckham had even ruffled their hair. Sam Hammam offered Alastair's son £20 to go and kick Beckham's ankles – one of Sam's standard jokes. The boy was most affronted, being a diehard Man. Utd fan.

Joe was the centre of attention in the boardroom, at least for all the Wimbledon directors and guests. A high court judge came up and asked him how he was, how they were missing him at Wimbledon, what were his plans now. Joe said he was looking forward to getting back into management.

'Anything lined up?' asked the judge.

'Got a few things in the air,' said Joe. 'Nothing definite yet, but I am coming back into football. Don't you worry.'

One of the players' wives came into the boardroom to give Joe a kiss. She said the new manger was more like a schoolteacher, sitting at his computer all day. There wasn't the emotion of involvement of Joe's days.

'Or the bollockings,' said Joe.

The wife of one of the directors came up and said how she too missed Joe. 'Oh I miss all of you as well,' Joe replied.

'I do miss the people here – Sam, David Barnard, Stanley Reed, David Kemp, Micky Harford, Terry Burton, Ron Stuart, Steve Allen, Roger Smith, Sid Neal, Joe Dillon, Ernie Tibbett. And of course I miss all the Crazy Gang – King Vinnie, Fash, Robbie, Wisey, Harts, oh and all the other Crazies. But you never know, I might be meeting some of them again. When I come back and buy them ...'

A waitress came up and asked Joe for his autograph. 'All the time you was here,' she said, 'I always forgot to ask you for it. Ten years, and I always forgot. Then you had your, er, thing. So I'm glad you've come back.'

'Good job I didn't die then,' said Joe, laughing, 'Then you'd never have got it.'

The season ended with Wimbledon being relegated. Would Joe have saved them, if he had been there? Who knows. But it illustrated, if further illustrations were needed, how much he had done for them during his years in charge.

In the close season, there was a further event with ironic overtones. Joe was offered the job as manager of Sheffield Wednesday – the club where he'd had his heart attack. He went up for three days, inspected their training ground, was most impressed by their facilities – but not by their financial situation. He concluded they would have to sell too many of their better players to survive. So he declined.

Will he come back? Or is that it, a distinguished career in football, as player and manager, brought to a sudden and unexpected end?

Perhaps by the time you read this he will be back, having begun a new chapter in his life. I hope so, for Joe's sake, and for football's sake. There are not many like Joe.

Joe Kinnear

Playing Career
Tottenham Hotspur

Season	Appearances	Div. One position
1965–66	8	8
1966–67	27	3
1967–68	37	7
1968–69	31	6
1969–70	13	11
1970–71	42	3
1971–72	32	6
1972–73	35	8
1973–74	14	11
1974–75	19	19

Total 1st team appearances: 258 (includes 7 as sub); 2 goals.

Honours:

FA Cup Final, 1967: Spurs 2, Chelsea 1

League Cup Final, 1971: Spurs 2, Aston Villa 0

UEFA Cup Final, 1972: Wolves 1, Spurs 2, Spurs 1, Wolves 1

League Cup Final, 1973: Spurs 1, Norwich 0

Brighton and Hove Albion
1975-77: 17 appearances

Republic of Ireland
1967-76: 26 caps

Management Career
Wimbledon

Season	Premier League position
1991–92	13 (Div. One)
1992–93	12
1993–94	6
1994–95	9
1995–96	14
1996–97	8
1997–98	15
1998–99	16

Cups:

FA Cup, 1996-97, lost in semi-final to Chelsea

League Cup, 1996-97, lost in semi-final to Leicester

League Cup, 1998-99, lost in semi-final to Spurs